WHAT HAPPENED ON

EASTER SATURDAY?

36HR MYSTERY BETWEEN DEATH AND RESURRECTION OF JESUS CHRIST

TRINITY ROYAL

What Happened on Easter Saturday?

36 hours Mystery between Christ death and Resurrection

Trinity Royal

Library of Congress Control Number: 2022920604

CONTENTS

Free books to our readers

War in Heaven came to Earth. Satan Rebellion:

https://dl.bookfunnel.com/ea12ys3dmk

Your Life in Heaven:

https://dl.bookfunnel.com/vg451qpuzs

INTRODUCTION

E aster Sunday is arguably the holiest day of the Christian year. While Christmas certainly has a special place, especially in the secular world, most devout Christian followers would point to Easter Sunday as the most holy celebrated day of their faith.

Such an important day has historical and liturgical precedence in the church. The 40 days leading up to Easter are known as the "season of Lent", which is a time of preparation for the death and resurrection of Christ. It is a somber season, and it begins with Ash Wednesday when we remember that we are dust and to dust, we shall return (Genesis 3:19).

Lent culminates in Holy Week, which starts with Palm Sunday, or in some traditions, Passion Sunday. The Sunday before Easter, this special day celebrates Jesus' triumphant entry into Jerusalem on a donkey. This story is one of the most familiar, as it is recounted in all four canonical gospels: Matthew, Mark, Luke, and John. It is seen as the high point of Jesus' earthly ministry, and it begins the holiest week of the Christian calendar.

Maundy Thursday is celebrated on the Thursday between Palm Sunday and Easter Sunday. It is remembered as the night Jesus gathered with His disciples in an upper room, and they shared a sacred meal that has become recognized today as the Communion Sacrament. Many churches hold Maundy Thursday services, honoring the Holy Eucharist and sharing in the sacred meal together.

Good Friday, so named for the good that came into the world through the sacrifice of Christ, is remembered next. It is the day that Christ was betrayed, arrested, put on trial, and ultimately the day He was crucified and died. Again, many churches hold special services, such as "The Seven Last Words", to share in remembrance of this ultimate sacrifice Christ gave for the salvation of this world.

Lastly, when Good Friday has come to its close, we move quickly on to Easter Sunday and the celebration of the Resurrection of Christ.

Yet, what happened on that Saturday? This book will explore that question and give it the answers it deserves.

Holy Saturday is known by many names including "Easter Saturday", "Black Saturday", "Easter Eve", and the "Great Sabbath". While it may have many titles, it is a holy day that is rarely, if ever, held in any sort of regard for most Christians.

The Holy Bible is clear, and the gospels attest to the narratives around Christ's death and resurrection. We know Jesus died on Good Friday and was resurrected on Easter Sunday, but we do not have the clearest picture of what happened on Holy Saturday.

To be sure, there are many contradictory opinions and teachings within the Christian community as to what happened on that fateful day nearly two millennia ago. This project does not aim to discredit and/or dissect any of those teachings.

The answers herein come from my own personal experience, intuition, guidance, and communications with higher beings. The sublime spectacle of the death of the human Jesus on the Cross of Golgotha has aroused the highest devotion of the angels and stirred the emotions and curiosities of mortals.

While Scriptures offer insight to theologians and historians as to what happened on this material plane, very few have an understanding of what transpired in the unseen realms during this great pause in the narrative of Christ.

Jesus' Bodily Form After the Resurrection

The various canonical gospels found in the Holy Bible give conflicting accounts as to what happened on Easter morning. Each of them tells different stories as to who, exactly, came to the tomb and to whom Jesus first appeared. Again and again, however, Jesus is not recognized by the disciples or Mary.

In John, Mary doesn't recognize him until Christ calls her by name. In Luke's account, a couple of the disciples walk with Jesus on the road to Emmaus. It isn't until Christ breaks bread with them, a ritual that recalls the Last Supper, that their eyes are opened, and they see Jesus for who he is.

Only in speaking and in sharing rituals is Jesus revealed to those with whom he was closest. This tells us that the physical body inhabited by Christ certainly is not the fully physical body he had before the Resurrection.

Not only that, but this new body is apparently capable of new phenomena that had been hitherto unseen. While Jesus's body was known for performing miracles, such as walking on water, His body after the Resurrection was capable of passing through walls. Multiple times, Jesus appears to the disciples while they are gathered in a locked room, and He has managed to appear and disappear from among them.

Although this tells us that Jesus' bodily form after the Resurrection is not fully physical, we also know it is not fully spiritual, either. Jesus had many encounters with His disciples and with other people in Judea around that time. Human senses cannot perceive the spirit body, as it is much more glorified and appears as almost entirely light with no form recognizable to the human eye.

The body Jesus inhabited was physical enough for Thomas to find the scars by putting his hands in the holes in Jesus' side. Additionally, Jesus Himself says, "Do not cling to me, I have not yet ascended [as a spirit] to the Father" (John 20:17).

These seemingly conflicting ideas of Jesus' body not being fully physical and not being fully spiritual beg the question: what bodily form does Jesus have after the Resurrection? This is a very important question that up until now has been neglected by scholarship and theology. You will find that answer and many more here.

In Summary:

- We know that Christ's body after the resurrection is not fully physical because:

  - His own disciples did not recognize him

  - He was recognized only when he spoke

  - He was able to walk through walls (appear and disappear)

- We know that Christ's body is not fully spirit body because:

  - Jesus, Himself said that He has not ascended as a spirit to the Father

  - Human eyes cannot see the spirit body

  - Spirit body is much more glorified and is 100% light with no form

  - Thomas would not have been able to find the scars in the spirit life form body

Which brings the question – **What body form does Christ have after the resurrection?**

This is a very important question. Let's dive in to find answers

Questions This Book Will Answer

1. Why did Christ resurrect on the third day instead of the first or second?

2. What happened in the Heavenly Realms on Holy

Saturday?

3. What happened on Earth with Jesus' family, the disciples, the witnesses of his death, and the Sanhedrin?

4. What happened to Jesus' physical body while it was in the tomb?

5. What happened in the Universal Realms immediately after Christ's death on the Cross?

6. What bodily form does Jesus have after the Resurrection, and why?

7. What happens to one's soul, spirit, memories, thoughts, and experiences after physical death?

8. How does the soul survive after physical death?

9. What happens in the first three days after physical death?

Who this book is for?

This book is for Christians who want to pursue the knowledge of what really happened in the 36 hours after Jesus' burial and before His resurrection. Of course, one does not need to be an avowed Christian in order to be a knowledge-seeker, a historian, or a theologian looking to deepen understanding of a historical event.

Anyone who is curious to know the truth of Jesus' death and resurrection, and those who want to expand their perspectives on life, death, and the existence of spiritual growth, will find this book invaluable.

It is important to say from the start that this book will delve into many words that are not found in the Scriptures, and for those who see any extra-biblical resources as blasphemy, this book may not be for you. However, my request is that you have an open mind to learning potentially new concepts. After all, if this topic is within normal human understanding, there already would have been many books in our libraries.

Additionally, I would say that this book isn't for nonspiritual people who have no interest in Christ or His mission. While you might learn facts and understanding, the real purpose of this project is to share a deeper comprehension of the spiritual self and how we should expect death and resurrection to be revealed to us as it was revealed through Christ.

Clarity at Last

There have been conflicting and confusing thoughts among theologians, scholars, and researchers ever since the Resurrection event itself. The intention of this book is not to say one such understanding is correct in its entirety or that another one is ill-informed.

This project promises to shed light on what occurred between Christ's death and resurrection here in the physical realm, what that means for us as followers of Christ who will surely come to know a physical death, and who expect a resurrection of the spiritual self.

While I do not claim to know it all, I humbly share findings based on research and personal experiences. It is my prayer that you find within these pages the clarity that has been lacking for so long in our understanding of what happened on Easter Saturday.

Let's jump in

We will open the book with Jesus' physical body being laid on the tomb. Then we will end with the Resurrection. Everything in-between is found in this book. Join me as we explore the 36-hour mystery between Christ's death and resurrection.

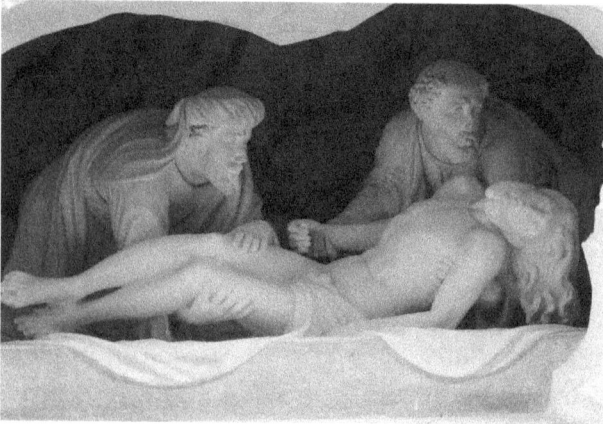

ROADMAP

B efore we start going down the path of enlightenment, let's look at the prevailing theories.

Prevalent Theories

There are other traditions that talk about what happened to Christ during this 36 hrs time in the tomb. Some contests that Jesus went to Hell, fought with Hades, and saved souls. This is actually one of the more common theories about what happened, but there is no factual basis for any of this story.

Similarly, in Mormonism, there is a belief that during this time, Jesus traveled to what would later become the United States to visit the lost tribe of Israel (the native people). Again, there is no actual proof or evidence, and does not align with what Jesus Himself said was going to happen.

I do not highlight these examples to downplay other people's faiths or religious beliefs but to share that there are alternative theories/ideas.

My hope is that by the end of this little book, you should have enough facts and knowledge to make a judgment yourself.

For those who follow Christ, it is your choice to know the truth of what happened during the Resurrection.

The Roadmap

Broadly there are two parts to this book. The first few chapters are basically laying the foundations. These foundations are the basic fabric of the universe. Depending on one's soul growth and spiritual maturity, the information may need to be digested.

Next, we will look at the components that make up a physical human being or any being and why it takes three days for the resurrection of a soul after death-sleep. We will look at what exactly happens immediately after death and why it takes that long. We will look at an example of why Christ did not raise Lazarus immediately but waited until after three days.

In the second part of the book, we will spend time looking at what exactly happened during the 36 hours while Christ's body lay inside the tomb. The physical body is still, but His Spirit is active. So what did His Spirit do?

When the women came to the tomb in early Sunday morning, they came into contact with beings of light, "men in dazzling white". Who are these non-physical visitors that came to visit our Saviour and what did they do?

I am excited and grateful to be part of this journey and to be able to bring this information to you. I sincerely hope your questions can be answered and that you can get something out of this.

WHAT IS HEAVEN?

These first few chapters will focus on some of the basics. We want to make sure we have a shared understanding of important words, concepts, and processes before diving into the more substantial subject matter of what happened to Christ's body on Holy Saturday.

Heaven may be something that a majority of people are familiar with, but I would urge you not to skip this chapter. Many people have different conceptions of Paradise, and everything from centuries-old poetry to modern Hollywood depictions of Heaven may leave us with incomplete or misguided ideas of what the Kingdom of God actually is.

As with the rest of this book, this chapter will look at Scripture as the basis for our understanding, but we will not end there. God's realms are too great to be captured in just a few books, so we will rely on a few, extra-Biblical notions to fill in the gaps. While it would take eons of writing to fully capture all that is to be expected in a concept of Heaven, for the purposes of understanding Christ's ordeal on Easter Saturday, we will focus on just a brief glimpse of Paradise.

The Presence of God

> "In my Father's house there are many dwelling-places. If it were not so, would I have told you that I go to prepare a place for you?"
> - Jesus (John 14:2)

The ultimate goal of any faith-based being is to be in the presence of God, sit at the Father's right hand, and become one with God. We see this across all religions, though most of the world's religions come up short in their understanding of who God is and what it means to be in the presence of God.

In both Mark's gospel (Mark 10:35-45) and Matthew's (Matthew 20:20-28), the disciple's John and James are fighting over who will be seated at Jesus' right hand in the Kingdom yet to come. Although there are differences in the two gospel narratives, Mark shows the disciples fighting amongst themselves, and Matthew tells of their mother intervening on their behalf and asking this favor of Jesus, the point remains the same. The disciples know there is great honor and glory that comes with being at the right hand of Christ in the Heavenly Realms.

This does, in fact, get them into a bit of trouble with the other disciples who are not too pleased that their comrades would be having such a discussion without them. They, too, know how important it is to be at Jesus' right hand and to be omitted from the conversation is insulting and upsetting to them.

Being in God's presence is exactly what Jesus is promising those who follow Him when He speaks the words quoted at the beginning of this section. It is not simply to go to a place where nothing bad happens or where everything is perfect all the time. The best we can imagine cannot even begin to come close to what spiritual ecstasy is in store for those who are able to dwell in the house of the LORD and to sit in His presence.

Jesus makes this promise and assures His followers that this is part of His purpose for His time on Earth. He needs to tell us this so we may know what is coming next and what we can expect if we lead a life worthy of Paradise.

There are many dwelling-places, meaning the Universe is big with a multitude of places (each having a different set of experiences). Heaven is not just one place but a multitude of places.

So, Where is God?

If we are wanting to be in God's presence, it would make sense to ask the question, "Where is God?"

We are a part of God's creation, as is all of the Universe. As the Universe expands, so, too, does Creation. God is still at work. In our small part of existence, people often claim to have experiences when they see God. Some people find God in the awesome power of nature, in the humbling love of a dear friend, in the beauty that can be seen in this life, and through so much more.

I am not seeking to diminish these experiences, but I do want to clarify that these are more like markers, a trail of breadcrumbs, if you will, to the reality of God's true awesomeness. These experiences are, in some ways, necessary for us to continue our pursuit of the Holy, and these glimpses of God sustain us for the journey that asks so much of us in our quest to follow Christ.

Still, where do these breadcrumbs lead? Where are the symbols pointing?

If followed faithfully, we come to find God at Paradise Isle. It is a singular place that is the abode of God the Father, God the Eternal Son, and God the Infinite Spirit.

The trails and symbols that lead us there are not easily followed on any sort of map or geographical understanding of the world. There are numerous levels of consciousness between the physical, material world we occupy and this deeper reality of Paradise Isle.

So, Where is Heaven?

In knowing that Paradise Isle is the place of true unity between God the Father, God the Eternal Son, and God the

Infinite Spirit, it follows that this place is a part of Heaven. Where then, is Heaven, you might ask?

Heaven, also, is a place, but it is not just one single place. It is a multitude of places. I know that may be difficult to understand, but the multiplicity of locations is due to the fact that the meaning and experience of Heaven are different depending on where one is at in their evolutionary journey.

For a material human being, such as you or me, every level beyond the immediate physical realm we occupy with our five senses is considered Heaven. For our basic, sensory bodies, even just taking one step beyond this plane is a step into a Heavenly Realm.

Just because we enter into a Heavenly Realm, however, does not mean we have come fully into the presence of God. If we imagined one step to be the entire journey, we would again be limiting the grandness and magnitude of God's great design of all that is and all that ever will be.

For a soul life-form and a spiritual life-form (which we will explore in depth in later chapters), the number of consciousness levels–or number of Heavens–is lesser.

It can help to imagine a target with a bull's eye in the center and concentric circles outward. Just being on the target means we have taken a step to exit this bodily plane and into the spiritual realm of Heaven. As we continue to move towards the center, our soul life-form and spirit life-form experience increased heavenly proximity.

The imagery of a target is, of course, an oversimplification. In reality, there is a very deliberate structure and order to creation that has been ordained since the dawn of time by the One who brings all things into being. There is precision, hierarchy, and order that have existed beyond our conceptions of time and space.

We come to know of this through the revelation of Jesus Christ and by following His teachings. Our education does not, however, end with our exit from this earthly plane. Rather, we are in a school of continuous evolution. The only constant in existence is change that leads to spiritual evolution and growth.

While this is the only true foundation of determining where Heaven is and how we can approach Paradise Isle, there are no simple shortcuts to reaching the center of the target.

It is impossible for us to be transformed as a creature of gross, animal nature into a perfected spirit by some sort of mysterious act of creative magic. The Creator's desire to produce a perfect being is done so by giving us the tools and understanding to develop ourselves into perfection. It takes our initiative and desires to reach heavenly perfection in order to move towards our ultimate goal of experiencing Paradise in the very presence of God.

THE VARIOUS LEVELS OF HEAVEN

The information included in the next two chapters is fairly advanced. It is a part of this book because it gives a complete picture of the different levels of Heaven as it relates to our location on the planet Earth.

It would only be natural if the previous chapters led to further questions about the ongoing development of the soul, the structure of Heaven and Earth, and what the other worlds outside of this one are made up of.

Depending on one's spiritual maturity, some concepts might be new. Please do not get too caught up in the difficulties and complexities of this chapter. If it feels like this is too advanced for you, feel free to skip it.

Heaven is a location, not a mind concept

Most of us have some concept of Heaven, even if it has been characteristically one formed by movies like *What Dreams May Come or The Lovely Bones*, or thinking it involves meeting as in the movie *Bruce Almighty*. Just as a movie requires a set direction and props, Heaven may just as well be similarly designed, but by one of the best designers, set directors, and make-up artists combined into One and by God Himself. It is created by "the One", the Father who brings all things into being. The many levels of Heaven are as deliberately designed as any stage or movie set and include an intentional structure and order to creation that has existed since the dawn of time. Most certainly when we come to understand that our very soul, spirit, and identity are equally quite remarkable, then it comes as no surprise that Heaven too is just as real and astounding a place as the rest of all creation. In this chapter, we will explore the basic physical structure of Heaven and the various levels this Kingdom possesses.

While we can dream and imagine the white puffy clouds as being pillows that tuck us into our angel feather beds at night, and eternal sunshine exists as our backdrop as we float through in the expansive blue sky each day, it's actually not like that! Rather, Heaven is an actual location and not a mind concept. As taught by Jesus, he said, "I go to prepare a place for you" (*New International Version*, 1973,

John 14:2). This place, Heaven, as told by Jesus, is prepared and planned. This intentionality of Heaven can set us at ease. We tend to put God in a box and try to explain with our limited conscious understanding what things are all about when in reality, God determines all, and we are only human after all. Imagine and allow for the incredible graces of our Holy Father to plan and have a dwelling place for us and know this to be true. When we can do this, the concept of Heaven becomes easily understandable and grasped as a relatable place that is waiting for us. The Father is loving and He has prepared for you a multitude of worlds on which you will continue to accumulate experience. It is simply impossible to gather all of the experiences of your soul's destiny in just one world, and only the initial one at that. When you have the path of the whole of creation laid down before you, with limitless experiences and boundless worlds, there are eternal structures you will see that will amaze you along your journey.

The Structure of Heaven

While you may be a beginner or have many years of growing and expanding your spiritual foundations on your relationship journey with God the Father, you may already know that Heaven is a place with multiple locations. We have established that it is not one single place but that the number of locations is varied and even infinite. For some, this may be common knowledge, whereas, for others, it may be a new concept. Regardless, bringing you the reader to this point of awareness and comprehension is key for this part of the book and for the remainder of the chapters as we will begin to traverse the physical structures of Heaven as well as our layers of consciousness to get there.

Be sure to go slow and take time to explore, understand, and integrate the following concepts that support ideas relating to the structure of Heaven, especially if some of these ideas may be new to you.

We can classify the structure of reality and worlds as categorized as layers into 3 broad categories that range from the material world being the most-dense to non-material as the least dense. Then there is Paradise where God, the deity resides.

1. Material worlds (physical worlds like Earth)

2. Semi-Material worlds (transition worlds, also called Morontia worlds)

3. Non-material worlds (Spirit Worlds)

4. Paradise (God's abode, beyond time and space)

The structure, makeup, and complexity of worlds increase as one moves from the lower to the higher dimensional levels not in physical complexity, but in their frequency. Imagine that each level corresponds with a dimension. The less dense we are in the material world, the higher the frequency in the less-dense dimension. And, the frequencies of higher dimensions are more complex than the ones below. Let me explain this further. If we were to place living beings in the most-dense material plane, it is easy to comprehend that the chemical composition and complexity of the level above is higher than the level below yet appears and is more physically dense. Higher levels or dimensions require less food or sustenance than a lower-level living being would consume but are more complex in frequency. Overall, it is therefore safe to assume that food or sustenance requirements will reduce as body-form frequencies increase.

Think of it in relation to the concept of vapor that rises without having form or density. The higher you go, the higher the senses become and less sustenance is required. At some point, experiences beyond the five senses will start to open. This can lead to the understanding that the abilities that people have in the higher Heavens are more complex than what we are accustomed to and may be represented through advanced telepathy or having other super-sensory skills or powers that equate with being generally common for that level or dimension. Forget the internet, imagine how fast messages could arrive if they were simply sent and received on a mental signal that didn't require opening up your email and reading it, let alone finding the "on" switch. The three worlds are broken down individually and outlined below and will clarify the different levels of existence to which our human body, soul, and spirit can experience after our earthly death sleep.

The Three Worlds of Space and Time

Material world (Physical worlds like Earth)

The material world is right outside your doorstep. We are fully aware of this earthly plane that can be felt by the ground that we walk upon, the seasons that change in our geographical locations, and the tides of the water that rise and fall with each phase of the moon. Each part of our Earth and its sphere is made up of certain chemical elements, for example, periodic table elements that all have certain vibrational frequencies that are not only found within our bodies but also the planet as a whole. For those who are familiar with the Shuman resonance, it acknowledges that "each lightning burst creates electromagnetic waves that begin to circle around Earth, captured between Earth's surface and a boundary about 60 miles up. Some of the waves—if they have just the right wavelength—combine, increasing in strength, to create a repeating atmospheric heartbeat known as Schumann resonance" (Wilson, 2013). These incredible electromagnetic waves are present around us and keep us in the earth's container, grounded in physicality and energetic impulses that make up and define the material world. The Earth, as we know it, also contains physical and dense beings—we humans—that require food and sustenance for our bodies. It is the food that we consume that fuels our own living energy and keeps our cellular structure, blood flow, and heartbeat alive, all maintained within the unique properties of this material dimension.

Semi-material worlds (Transition worlds also called Morontial worlds)

While Earth is a planet with a density we are certainly familiar with where we can walk, drive, and even fly in an airplane as part of our experience, what are the semi-material or transition worlds? *Morontia* is a term that refers to the vast level suspended between the material and the non-material (spiritual planes). There are many sub-levels within this realm. Each *Morontia* world is characteristically more refined, complex, and considerably less dense than the one below it. While knowledge or even awareness of these worlds is not very common or well-known to most people, they are documented in the Bible.

One of Jesus' own disciples wrote about an 'enduring substance' of Heaven that can lead one to contemplate the existence of the *morontial* worlds, as it is written in Hebrews; "For ye had compassion of me in my bonds, and took joyfully the spoiling of your goods, knowing in yourselves that ye have in heaven a better and an enduring substance." (*King James Bible*, 2017/1769, Hebrews 10:34). As you rise in these semi-material worlds, they become less dense and, according to this biblical reference, existence has a more timeless frequency that may be best measured and described as immortality. Once we begin to transcend the earthly realm, vibrational frequencies increase, and the spaces contain beings who are less dense and whose bodies need less food and sustenance for survival.

While it may be strange to think of beings other than humans who live in other dimensions and these angelic or other beings of reference are new to you, these beings living here have a body form technically called *Soul Body*. When Christ was resurrected, Christ's body was a *Soul Body* form. This is semi-material. If it was not, doubting Thomas would not have been able to touch the wounds of Jesus Christ whose biblical story demonstrates the importance of believing and having faith; "then he said to Thomas, 'Put your finger here, and see my hands; and put out your hand, and place it in my side. Do not disbelieve but believe.' Thomas answered him, 'My Lord and my God!' Jesus said to him, 'Have you believed because you have seen me? Blessed are those who have not seen and yet have believed'" (*New International Version*, 1973,). Not only does this story represent the power of faith during the time of Jesus' resurrection, but the form of Jesus' body was a *Soul Body*. If His body was fully spirit, He would not have a form to be recognized by the apostles during His resurrection. Many did not recognize Him at first glance, unless He revealed Himself, meaning He did not have a pure physical body. When we begin to imagine the spaces beyond our physical and material world, and the impermanence of our life and our own physical body, it clarifies how incredible our own human body is and the fact that a Soul Body and other creatures exist is entirely fathomable. Perhaps it is when we acknowledge the spiritual world and complete transcendence that many begin to scratch their heads and wonder if spiritual ascension is feasible. This semi-material world may introduce some notions of Soul Body and impermanence, but it is the spirit worlds that take us to yet a higher frequency even more astounding.

Non-material Worlds (Spirit worlds)

The spirit worlds might be easier to imagine if you have spent time watching science fiction movies of mythical realms and creatures that walk on other planets. While you witness and experience the visuals of these places through colorfully filmed productions, the spiritual world, distinct from the physical world, can be perceived just as incredible. But true depictions of the spiritual world may not be entirely possible due to subjective realities and our lack of ability to perceive them. I will do my best here to describe these spaces of the spiritual world that may not elude all of us. According to the best of my knowledge and experience, there are numerous spirit worlds. As we can best imagine they are different from the material world grounded in the earth. The spirit worlds have energy wavelengths and celestial bodies that require food and substance yet at a much lesser frequency. The spirit is 100% light and therefore there is no substance to the body form. There is no need for food or sustenance for the celestial beings that are 100% light because the spirit is self-generating. It is possible that many beings who are from spirit worlds came to Earth as planetary teachers and are walking among us.

If you can imagine the spirit as light, then it is possible to comprehend that the vibrations of a spirit being is very high, meaning that their frequency operates not on the dense emotions of fear, hate, or sorrow as an example, but contains more love, joy, and gratitude. Aside from the amount of information that we can find on the internet these days, presently and historically we have seen pictures of these celestial beings with halos around their heads, like those of Christ, and maybe even floating above in the air. I believe this represents a self-generating glow of Spirit. This representation of divinity or beings of divine stature is celestial beings who live in the spirit worlds that surround us and exist on different dimensions. The spirit world is a level that is one dimension lower than Paradise, the abode of the Holy God, the deity.

Paradise – God's abode

The best possible attempt to describe and define God's abode and utilize the most appropriate English word possible would be *Paradise*. This place isn't referring to the five-star hotel situated on the turquoise oceanfront property of a tropical island that we may dream about but, if you set your imagination on a place that is uniquely unfathomable to our limited consciousness, you might just be able to comprehend it. Why is the word "Paradise" appropriate to refer to Heaven? When understanding the origin of the word Paradise from early English, French, and Latin, it has interestingly enough been directly translated as 'The Garden of Eden' (Etymonline, 2022). This makes this choice of the word quite appropriate, it appears, as it relates to the book of Genesis as one of the first Books in the Bible. The Garden of Eden "is the story of the heavens and the Earth when they were made, in the day the Lord God made the Earth and the heavens" (*New International Version*, 1973, Genesis 2:4-6). Paradise is used frequently throughout the Bible including in the book of Luke when it says, "and Jesus said unto him. Verily I say unto thee, Today shalt thou be with me in paradise" (*New International Version*, 1973,). Paradise is the dwelling place of the Trinity—God the Father, God the Eternal Son, and God the Infinite Spirit—and conjures many ideal qualities to define the Heavenly Kingdom.

Paradise is the indwelling place of all beings and is where God himself resides in the Kingdom of all eternity. When a person dies, the soul and, as we addressed in earlier chapters, the spirit detaches and goes to Paradise to be in the presence of God. If we can suspend the limitations of our human consciousness momentarily, we may be able to grasp the infinite concept of this resurrected place referred to as Paradise. We can identify it as a place that has no time and exists in one eternal moment. Since everything created has movement, for example, the planets, stars, sun, and galaxies that are in constant motion and so in tune with the expansiveness of the universe and unequivocal harmony, there is another end of the spectrum. It is possible to imagine that no time or space can exist either. Can you imagine it? Can you resonate with both perspectives of the duality of the existence within our universe created by God? Is it possible to comprehend or exist in absolute movement and utter stillness while being in a timeless place where God exists in all realms with an eternal presence? Many do believe this is possible.

In my other book series related to Heaven, I have discussed the structure of Heaven, its different levels, and generally what do life in Heaven look like. If you are interested in this fascinating topic, please check out my other books.

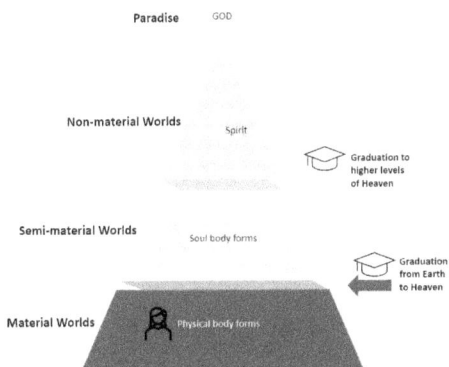

WHAT IS THE NORMAL
EVOLUTIONARY PROCESS?

N ow that we understand we are in a state of constant evolution, it is helpful to know what that process normally looks like. This chapter will explore those phases in broad terms. Again, like the chapter concerning Heaven, some of the languages that is used may be presumed to be familiar to us. Still, it is important to read thoroughly so we can have a greater shared understanding of words like 'soul' and 'spirit'.

Often, people will use such words interchangeably. Perhaps this works for poets, but if we are being serious about our understanding of Heaven and the evolutionary process of our true selves, then we need to have distinctions between these words and a knowledge of what is meant when we speak about these different pieces of ourselves on the journey.

This normal process will be essential to understand when we later examine Christ's experience after His death on Good Friday and before His resurrection on Easter Sunday. To know how He deviated from the normal transition and chain of events, we must know what the normal path entails.

To be clear, this is only a brief outline and an understanding of deeper realms that serves our purpose in gaining clarity to what Christ went through on Holy Saturday. There are many sublevels within the forms of soul and spirit, which certainly merit thought and consideration, but are ultimately erroneous for the goals of this book. If we dig too deep into the details, we may miss the big picture.

The Life-Forms

Our physical, soul, and spiritual life-forms are all distinctly different parts of the same whole that makeup who we are. Of course, we are most familiarly acquainted with our physical selves, so I won't spend too much time talking about what makes up our physical bodies. Although we think we know ourselves, it is important to understand *how* our physical bodies relate to our soul and spiritual life-forms.

The way that one can determine the difference between the physical, soul, and spiritual life-forms is through vibration frequencies. As these frequencies increase, the body is capable of holding more light and energy, which is needed to transcend to the higher Heavenly Realms. This will all be made clear as we examine each of the life-forms and their unique characteristics.

The Physical Life-Form

The physical self is only equipped to see material life-forms. This means that our senses are only made to perceive this physical world we occupy currently. We cannot see, hear, smell, taste, or touch soul or spirit life-forms.

Material life-forms, like our physical bodies, are base, animal bodies. Our vibrational frequencies are very low, and the materials that make up our bodies are very dense. We lack the spiritual evolution to be able to determine our frequencies and have no potential for carrying light in these bodies, so, we do not. This is why we are yet to experience any of the Heavenly Realms.

However, there are always exceptions. There are many stories in Eastern religions where Sadhus and Rishis were able to raise vibrations temporarily and disappear and reappear at will. This comes with a great amount of spiritual growth and penance.

While this is rare, it is sufficient to know it is possible.

The Spiritual Life-Form

The spiritual life-form is much less dense than the material life-forms. It has a much higher vibrational frequency as well, which facilitates much more light. A pure spiritual being is 100% light. There is no form to spirit body-forms.

While material life-forms cannot see spiritual beings, the same thing is not true in reverse. Spiritual life-forms can manifest in the physical by reducing vibrations and matching the levels that are needed for visibility in the material realm.

For example, there are many holy texts that attest to angels interacting with mortals. When the Archangel Gabriel came to speak to Mary who is in material-form, (Luke 1:26) he did so by reducing his vibration to physical, earth-vibration frequency, and only then could Mary's physical eyes was able to perceive the Archangel Gabriel. Only then could her ears hear his words and she was able to receive the news that she was to be the one to bear the Christ.

While these physical appearances are easy for spiritual life-forms, it can be difficult for those of us in the material world. The spiritual life-form, though visible and audible to our senses, still appears as a glow of light or a shadow of some form. Usually, there is not a denseness that would be familiar to our world.

The difficulty lies in the physical life-forms' openness to receiving the truth presented by spiritual beings. Often, if we are unreceptive, it is necessary for the spiritual being to appear in a dream.

Again, this is easy for a spiritual life-form to do, but sometimes it is easier for material life-forms to perceive and understand. "I was asleep, but my heart was awake!" (Song of Solomon 5:2). This manifestation happens to prophets like Jeremiah and Daniel and men like Joseph.

Spiritual life-forms do not require food or sleep. Their energy is derived from within. As mentioned before, there are varying levels and gradations within the spiritual form, but for our purposes, it is only important to know that a pure spirit is 100% light, and God is also 100% light.

The Soul Life-Form

The material body-form is dense carrying less light capacity whereas spirit body is 100% pure light and has no substance to it. A being cannot directly go from material body to spirit-infused body of 100% light directly; it is analogous to going from zero-mph to 1000-mph instantaneously. This is not practical. There is precision, hierarchy and order in the creation. Evolution is a progression.

There is a body form very common in lower levels of heaven. This is known as the soul life-form (also known as the "Morontia Life-Form"). This is a kind of liaison between the physical, bodily form we occupy now and the fullest form of the spiritual self.

Soul life-forms have a greater vibrational frequency than the physical body, but not the full potential of frequencies that will be realized at the spiritual level. While the soul life-form is not yet the spiritual one, it is still a being that can experience Heaven, albeit just the outer realms.

The soul life-form is the necessary step for the physical being to take. A physical being cannot simply raise its vibrations and pass into the spirit level. Only through evolution and growth does it achieve the soul life-form as a crucial step towards the spiritual self.

It is important to understand this body because it is the one Christ chose for His 40 days on Earth after Holy Saturday. This form allows for easier reception and clarity at the material level. Since Christ was spending those 40 days in contact with humanity on this earthly plane, the soul level made the most sense for his apparition.

While physical life-forms cannot normally see soul life-forms, it is important to know that the latter are able to see and interact with the physical realm. They do so by lowering their vibrational frequencies and becoming dense enough to be perceived by human senses.

There is some natural substance to the soul life-form that allows for the denseness required to be seen in the material plane as something other than pure light (as we'll see shortly with spiritual beings). The advantage of this form is that it is easily sensed by humans due to having sufficient substance in the physical world, which was essential for the purposes of Jesus' time on Earth during the 40 days after Holy Saturday.

Jesus Rose on the Third Day

Time and time again throughout the gospels, Jesus tells His disciples that He will be put to death, but on the third day, He will rise again.

Often we read about how the disciples do not understand this. To be sure, there is a lot that the disciples do not understand, and it is clear they do not expect Jesus' resurrection to come Easter Sunday. There is, however, more to it than that simple lack of believing the actual words Jesus says.

The truth is that the disciples didn't know the process. Christ knew it would take time to pass through to the soul and spiritual life-forms. When a being ascends from the physical to the soul or from the Soul life to the spiritual life, it retains all of the personal memories of the former and lower existences.

In that way, it takes a day or more for the spirit to reflect on its journey, take rest, recuperate, and raise frequencies to the appropriate levels for advanced existence. Similarly, by going back and forth between the soul-body existence, the spiritual-body, and back to the Soul-body plane, it takes time appropriate for these shifts in form changes. Resurrection cannot be rushed and can only happen when proper transitions between these life-forms take place.

"DEATH SLEEP": WHAT HAPPENS TO A PERSON'S PHYSICAL BODY?

For the perishable must clothe itself with the imperishable, and the mortal with immortality. When the perishable has been clothed with the imperishable, and the mortal with immortality, then the saying that is written will come true: "Death has been swallowed up in victory." "Where, O death, is your victory? Where, O death, is your sting?" (1 Corinthians 15:54)

D eath comes for us all. We know, that apart from taxes, it is the only certainty in this life.

Jokes aside, we are aware that this life is surrounded by death, and ultimately, we will all come to know death.

Death can be thought of as a kind of separation. You may have heard of someone saying that an estranged relationship is "dead to me." Of course, this means they are so separated that the love that once was there between the two is now gone, and the person might as well be dead. It is a statement regarding the level of separation. This is just a saying, but it helps to understand death as a separation.

Physical death is the separation of our body from our soul or spirit, while spiritual death is the separation of our soul from God. Jesus taught us that we do not need to have fear of physical death, but our concern should be with the potential of spiritual death.

When Paul writes in 1 Corinthians about death being swallowed up and no longer has its sting, it is a reference to the physical death being inconsequential in light of the pathways to move forward into the soul and spiritual realities of our bodies. Jesus' ministry on Earth gives us the way forward into those possibilities that were not previously available to us.

> Ephesians 2:8 tells us that, "For by grace you have been saved through faith, and this is not your own doing; it is the gift of God." (NRSV)

By faith in Christ, we have the potential to move forward, which means that physical death loses any power over us. If, however, a person has no faith, their identity is usually dissolved, and their being ceases to exist.

Due to Lucifer's Rebellion and Earth turning into a planet of imprisonment, our world has become very complicated. Souls are trapped here and are not permitted to continue on to the journeys promised to an eternal soul. This complication is circumvented in part through Christ's life, death, and resurrection, but there is still a requirement of our own spiritual evolution.

We will steer clear of reincarnation for now, though this concept ought not to be neglected in its entirety. It is not something that pertains to our understanding of what Christ went through, but it is understandable to have questions as to how this concept may or may not impact our own spiritual journeys.

With faith in Christ, we come to know that physical death is just a transition to a new form of existence, which leads to eternal life, incessant adventure, spiritual fulfillment, and unending service. We move in this way because we are created with the will to find God and to be in union with Him eventually. This is the basis of all spiritual evolution.

The Resurrection of Identity After Material Death

Generally, the person experiences a kind of resurrection after the material death. As mentioned in the previous chapter, the ascending self maintains all personal memories and has to take time to process the transition, changing vibrational frequencies, and densities to allow for a full shift into a new life-form.

Christ's resurrection is, of course, an exception that we will examine in-depth in the second part of this book. To understand how much of an exception this is and how Jesus' experience was such a departure from the norm, it is important to know what the established process is in the order of the Universe.

When a person of faith dies in the material world, what dies is their material being. The identity of the person, meaning the soul, and spirit (or thought-adjuster) of the person is collected and protected by specially-designed Seraphim angels whose only purpose is this. These 'Seraphim' are not the humans with wings you might be picturing from some artwork or stained-glass church windows. These designated Seraphim cannot be seen by material eyes as they have the soul-body form.

These Seraphims are specifically designated beings who are entrusted to care for the soul of the being after the death sleep. These beings of light have the capability to protect the soul with-in themselves as they journey through to the heavenly worlds.

At this point of death, the spirit disengages and is free. What exactly happens is not fully known, though my humble assumption is that the spirit goes into the presence of God. Christ's final words were spoken to God the Father when He said, "I commend my spirit into your hands..." (Luke 23:46). This means that the Spirit after death goes to God immediately after disengaging from the material body.

The spirit carries with it all of the memories, thoughts, and experiences of the self. In other words, the identity of the person is held within the spirit. My assumption is that this identity travels to the very presence of God as part of the resurrection and awareness of the various vibrational and density levels of the self.

The identity, having gone as far as it can go, returns so that the great resurrection can begin on the next heavenly world (also known as Morontia worlds).

Time and Space in Heavens

Heaven is a location (not a mind concept), so every location has time and space. The time/space in heaven is much different than what we are used to in the physical. Does heaven have night and day? The answer depends on the level of heaven. In spirit realms, there is no night and day as the spirit is self-sustained and spirit-body-form does not need time to recuperate; however, in soul-body-forms (or Morntia levels) there is night and day. The soul-body is partly material and will need some level of sustainment.

Making along story short, one day in Soul-body form is equivalent to approx 3 days of Earth time. One day of Spirit-body form is like 1000 years of Earth time. Ancient scripture of Eastern tradition also alludes to this fact. There are multitude of levels of Heaven and so the time/space is different at each level.

Note: I have discussed a bit more details of Heaven and time/space characteristics in my upcoming book series "Heaven". For this short book, i think this understanding will suffice.

The Third Day

Seraphim that are entrusted to protect the soul, bring that level of the self to meet with the spirit upon its return from God head. Although the exact manner of this reunion is not known, it is assumed that either God takes action at the moment or the spirit brings back new knowledge from being in the presence of God that facilitates this union.

Advisors and form creators, who carry out the will of God, make a suitable, Soul-body form that reflects the characteristics, personality, and vibrational patterns of the soul to make this body form compatible with the in-dwelling Soul and Spirit. This is unique to each and every one.

A fusion takes place between the soul and the spirit during this resurrection process. This is how all faith-based souls are resurrected and is the only process that has existed for eternity for every soul that has been saved from the material to the nonmaterial forms.

With this new identity, there are a number of things that can happen to the spirit. While we know that thoughts, memories, and experiences are stored permanently in the spirit, there is a necessary filtration of thoughts and memories that no longer serve a purpose at this level.

Jesus uses the language of separating the chaff from the wheat (Matthew 3:12) when describing how the Kingdom of God comes into being. Most often, this is understood to be a separation of the faithful from those who have no faith. This may be true, but the deeper truth is there are parts of our identities that are no longer needed upon reaching a Heavenly Realm, and they, too, are separated out as wheat and chaff.

There is not, however, a separation of good or bad seeds. These seeds are part of the very formation of a being's identity, and so, they cannot—and should not—be filtered out at this point.

The identity as a whole is preserved exactly as it was in the physical realm without, of course, the weight of physical limitations. The issues that one had while in physical like physical ailments and mental and emotional issues disappear. Bible says there is no sorrow on Earth that Heaven cannot heal. This is what this means.

There are also new memories of the soul and spirit that are formed in the Heavenly (or Morontial) realm that will carry forward with the being even if it moved back into the physical realm of existence.

Scripture attests to the existence of the soul-body forms and the reality of Heavenly (or Morontial) materials when Paul says:

"They have in heaven a better and more enduring substance" (Hebrews 10:34).

Understandably, all of this that has been shared in this chapter can seem deep and complex. If it feels overwhelming, please do not worry. The most important thing to know is that it takes three days after physical death to be translated into a soul life-form reunited with the spiritual self after its initial departure, ready to be resurrected from the Heavenly world with memories, thoughts, and spirit intact.

What Happened on Saturday - Christ's Associations

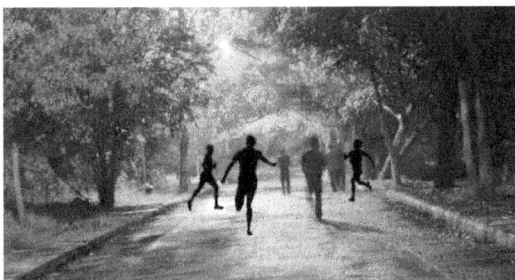

N ow that we have a shared understanding of what happens to the self after we experience material death, we can begin to explore the events of what happened 2,000 years ago when Christ's physical body died on the Cross. We will look, not only at what happened to Christ but also what happened to His associates as well.

The gospel narratives depict Jesus not as an isolated leader, but as someone who is constantly surrounded by community. He travels and preaches with His disciples, He has a family, He confronts religious leaders, and ultimately, He is sentenced to death by Pilate. This chapter will look at what happened with all of those people on Easter Saturday.

A reader may be curious as to why we will look at these individuals, but let us not forget we are people as well.

We have been given the same teachings and lessons as the disciples, and like them, we also have lacked the wisdom and understanding of what has actually happened to Christ.

We look at these human experiences so that we may find ourselves. Are we afraid of what we may learn? Are we confident in what we already know? Are we open to seeing beyond the empty tomb and into the Heavenly Realms of understanding?

There are many archetypes in the sacred scriptures, and each mortal-life experience gives us a chance to understand ourselves better so that we may gain in our self-awareness. May we learn from the mistakes of the disciples and those who were closest to Jesus so that we can more effectively begin to comprehend this physical realm and how to transcend it when the time comes.

Disciples or Apostles

As a quick note, you may often see the terms 'disciple' and 'apostle' as interchangeable. While they are similar, there is a big difference that matters in understanding who these early men were.

A 'disciple' is one who is *called*, while an 'apostle' is one who is *sent*. The 12 disciples were called to follow Jesus, and (in the course of their time with Him, but especially after His ascension) they were also sent out to do works in Jesus' name.

The distinction here matters mostly in understanding, that at the time of Jesus' death, the disciples had been called and spent some of their time being sent to towns on Jesus' behalf to share the good news (Luke 10:1), but their identities were still as followers and not yet as ones being sent out.

The disciples were those who were closest to Jesus. In various gospel accounts, we read of their calling and how Christ gathered them to be fishers of men (Mark 1:17). They were fishermen, tax collectors, professionals, sons, brothers, and the first followers of Christ.

John, James, Peter, Andrew, Bartholomew or Nathan, James the Lesser, Judas, Jude, Matthew, Phillip, Simon, and Thomas were the first 12 disciples. Many of them are familiar names to those who are acquainted with the Scriptures. For many, though, names such as 'Bartholomew' and 'Jude' may not be easy to recall from Sunday-school lessons.

We know that on Good Friday, Simon Peter, perhaps the most famous of the disciples, was the one who denied Christ three times before the cock crowed (Mark 14:30).

We know that Judas Iscariot, the most infamous of the 12, was the one who betrayed Christ at the hands of the authorities. He went on to hang himself (Matthew 27) after throwing the pieces of silver he had received as payment for turning Jesus over to the temple leaders who had bribed him.

Judas, of course, was a disciple but is not considered an apostle because he never went out to spread the good news of Christ after the Resurrection and Ascension. He was later replaced by Mattias, (Acts 1:21-26) who became the 12th apostle.

Other than the specific stories of Simon Peter and Judas, we do not know how the disciples individually spent their time on Good Friday and in the time immediately following Jesus' arrest and crucifixion.

We do know, however, what they did as a collective whole. With the exception of Judas, the disciples spent their time in hiding. They separated voluntarily out of fear of being captured. Their fear dictated their actions instead of their faith in Christ's words and explanations.

Jesus' brutal death frightened the disciples. They would have been known for associating so closely with the man, and undoubtedly, some of them may have been recognized as being a part of his cohort if they had gone out into the city. They did not think it was safe to leave.

The disciples had just witnessed their leader of the past three years be crucified for what He did and taught. As His closest followers, they felt as though they were criminals in Jerusalem and that it was not safe for them to be seen. Had they been caught, they might have also been put to death. They were still afraid of the death of the physical body.

Interestingly, they would later reverse this trend, with 11 of the 12 disciples dying a martyr's death, no longer afraid of the bodily death sleep, as they were safe in the knowledge of the resurrection that was promised to them. On Easter Saturday, however, they did not yet know this to be true.

Instead of living their faith, unafraid of what this world may do to them, they cowered in fear. Their shepherd had died, and the sheep were scattered.

Although Jesus had told them clearly many times what would happen, the disciples felt abandoned by God and left alone to fend for themselves. Their human ego had triumphed over their higher soul and spiritual selves, and their base, animal instincts got the better of them. The disciples spent Easter Saturday consumed by their fear.

Jesus' Family and Friends

While we know that Jesus was born of the Virgin Mary, and that His earthly father was Joseph, we often forget to mention His broader family. Jesus had siblings (though not related by blood to Him). James, Joses (Joseph), Simon, and Jude were his brothers, and Mary and Salome were his sisters. Some of this is attested to in the Book of Mark, and other components are filled in by historians of early Palestine.

Of the whereabouts of his family, we know that Jesus' mother was a witness to the crucifixion. Most of us cannot imagine the pain of losing a child, made all the more traumatic by witnessing the brutal and violent death of the child. Jesus' family was in utter pain and misery.

We know that Mary held so much in her heart and knew Jesus was destined for greatness through the annunciation given to her by the Archangel Gabriel at the beginning of Luke's gospel. Still, she and her family were in complete turmoil at the loss of their beloved family member.

There were also many women who were associated with Jesus' ministry. Mary Magdalene was perhaps the most well-known, but multiple gospels attest to many women being at the site of Jesus' crucifixion and ready on Easter Sunday for the anointing of the body.

In the Scriptures, we read of Mary Magdalene, Mary the wife of Clopas, Martha, another sister of Jesus' mother, and Rebecca of Sepphoris, who came with spices to prepare Jesus' body for its burial in accordance with Jewish ritual.

Some of the women who were at the crucifixion on Friday were ready on Sunday for the burial. That means they spent Saturday preparing. It is not always easy to have burial spices available. They must have met with family members or friends who could have sold or lent them the necessary spices and oils for the burial rites.

These women would also have known deep grief, but they felt they had a duty to carry out according to the laws of their religious customs. As such, their focus became centered on carrying out those laws to the best of their abilities.

Even devout people who want to do the right thing are still not fully capable of understanding the transformation Jesus is undergoing on Saturday. While the family and friends of Jesus are not afraid like his disciples, they are still blinded to the truth. They put their religious devotion ahead of their spiritual understanding, and as such, they are blind to the deeper reality of the resurrection.

Religious and Political Leaders

According to Matthew 27:62-66, we read: "*The next day, that is, after the day of Preparation, the* chief priests and the Pharisees gathered before Pilate and said, 'Sir, we remember what that impostor said while he was still alive, "After three days I will rise again." Therefore command that the tomb be made secure until the third day; otherwise his disciples may go and steal him away, and tell the people, "He has been raised from the dead", and the last deception would be worse than the first.' Pilate said to them, 'You have a guard of soldiers; go, make it as secure as you can.' So they went with the guard and made the tomb secure by sealing the stone." (NRSV)*

It is interesting that the religious leaders whom Jesus so often quarreled with would take his words more seriously than the disciples. While they may not have completely believed or grasped the meaning of Jesus' words, they were nonetheless paying attention to what Christ said and decided to take action to make sure it would not even appear to be true.

The religious leaders mentioned here were known as the 'Sanheidren' and were a kind of supreme council of Jewish religious authorities, including the high priest, Caiaphas. Jesus' death was a part of their plan because they saw Christ as a threat to their authority.

Of course, they were thinking only of the physical realm, and what little power they had that was delegated to them by the Roman Empire was paltry compared to the possibility of spiritual liberation. They did not know or care to know the depths of the soul, however, and made plans only benefiting themselves in the physical life body.

Pilate was okay siding with the religious leaders. He had even more authority and power than the Sanheidren but was untroubled by Jesus' life and teachings. He did not see Jesus as a threat, but he did see the possible trouble that could be stirred up by having a large conflict in the territory over which he was to govern.

We read of Pilate as being somewhat conflicted. In Matthew's gospel, we see Pilate constantly trying to give Jesus a pathway that leads away from the crucifixion. There is a part of Pilate that seems to know this is not right. Still, it is not enough for him to intervene completely. He does not speak up for Jesus and ultimately is the one who puts Christ to death.

On Easter Saturday, he agrees with the Sanhedrin, who requests the soldiers be sent to the tomb and even encourages sending an additional set of guards to make sure Jesus' body will be untouched by his followers.

These religious and political authorities are only concerned with their own power and influence. They may acknowledge the truth of Christ, but only inasmuch as it may threaten their own status. Some people can see Jesus' real teachings but know that to follow him spiritually will lead to a sacrifice of all they have gained in their physical life body. Rather than believing that the soul and spiritual self can achieve deeper truths, they put Christ and his teachings to death in a vain attempt to preserve what little earthly power they may have.

What Happened on Saturday - The Unseen Heavenly Realm

UNBELIEVABLE SILENCE

T here is no way to fully capture the totality of the reaction of the heavenly beings to Jesus' death on the Cross.

All of us in this life have brushes with death. Our friends and our family come and go. With any sort of luck and a lot of prayers, our loved ones grow to old age and pass away in peace.

We know death comes for us all, and still, it can often be incredibly difficult to really come to terms with the notion.

Jesus knew He would die. He had been explaining it to His disciples in the time leading up to His crucifixion. It was known, not only on Earth but also in the Heavenly Realms.

Those beings who had been with God the Creator since the beginning were aware of the blueprint.

Perhaps they did not know all of the details. God most certainly held back information that was not necessary for those angelic beings to have. Still, they knew that part of Jesus' time on Earth would be His death, and ultimately, His resurrection.

Just as we may know a loved one is soon to pass away, we are still grieved when they actually die.

Orphaned Universe

At the moment Jesus breathed His last, the angels collectively gasped. Their jaws dropped to the floor in disbelief, and their hearts ripped asunder like the curtain in the temple (Matthew 27:51) when Jesus died.

The Beloved of the Universe, the Creator of the Heavenly Realms died. Not only did He die, but He was killed a violent and ignoble death. **The creatures killed their Creator**.

At their core, the angelic beings knew that this would be a part of the plan, but they may still have questioned in their hearts why God would go through so much pain for the sake of humanity. God certainly did not have to come as Christ and even more so did not need to endure the humiliation and suffering of death on the Cross. Yet, He did.

The Universe held its breath in silence, in terrible awe of the death of its Beloved. For a brief moment in time, the Universe became orphaned. There was a creation without a creator, a kingdom without a king, and the Ruler of the Universe was no more.

This moment is known as the **"Great Silence"**. Even God the Father is silent in Paradise. Knowing the truth of the coming resurrection does not erase the pain of losing a child and knowing what He endured in death.

The streets of Salvington, the city-like headquarters of the Universe, came to a complete stop. All activity ceased as though a movie were paused and no one could move. No one could fathom movement. What is there to go on for if the Creator of the Universe has been put to death?

Even Gabriel and Melchizedek, the two light beings who spoke to Jesus in the garden of Gethsemane prior to the crucifixion, were concerned and silent. We know that the memorial on Earth is coming soon, but there is a quiet reverence yet to be had for the unfolding of the greatest drama in the Universe.

These powerful beings of light have the ability to step in and change the course of events. They could have interfered on Christ's behalf easily. They could have put a stop to the ugliness of the crucifixion. Yet, they did not. They were not directed to do so by God the Creator, and so they did nothing. Still, their hearts ached as all they could do was sit and watch on in silence.

Our human hearts know grief. We know anger. We know pain, suffering, and loss. Ultimately, however, we still have human hearts with limitations. We cannot even hope to begin to conceive of the indignation that swept over the vast wholeness of the Universe.

The Celestial Intelligentsia, those who had become pure light through the awareness of true salvation and the raising of their frequencies to become beings of truth, have just been witnesses to their beloved sovereign submitting Himself to the will of the ignorant and misguided creatures on the sin-darkened sphere of Earth.

On Easter Saturday, the Universe was orphaned.

Meanwhile, Inside the Tomb...

Christ's spirit returned on Saturday from being with God. The spirit has come to be in the tomb, but it has not yet entered the physical body.

The spirit is at work summoning other beings.

> Melchizedek, an Ancient of Days, spoke to Jesus. In the Book of Truth, Jesus is quoted as telling them, "*Having finished my life in the flesh, I would tarry here for a short time in transition from that I may more fully know the life of my ascendant creatures and further reveal the will of my Father in Paradise.*"

Meanwhile, the Archangel Gabriel was placed temporarily in charge of universal affairs and maintaining the order of the Creator. Plenty of help was offered from heavenly beings of all kinds, as the Universe worked together for the good of God.

WHAT HAPPENED ON
SATURDAY - CHRIST HIMSELF

In Chapter 5, there was an opportunity for us to see our response to Christ's death. Are we scared and scattered like the disciples, lacking faith and understanding? Are we, like Jesus' family, overwhelmed with grief and channeling our feelings into misguided, religious devotion instead of a faithful following of Christ's deeper spiritual self? Are we, like the religious and political authorities, afraid of what Jesus is teaching us because it threatens our way of enjoying the physical life body?

No matter who you are or how you have looked at Easter Saturday before, this chapter is a chance for you to explore what Jesus went through so you can gain an understanding, channel your response in a spiritually-appropriate direction, and live without attachment to this physical realm.

After Jesus was crucified, his physical body was taken off of the cross and laid in the tomb, which was then sealed with a great stone, and guards were stationed outside. We know this from the gospel accounts and multiple attestations to Jesus' death in extra-biblical narratives as well.

Much more happened within the dark walls of the tomb. We are so quick in Christian tradition to skip from Good Friday to Easter Sunday, but we need to pay attention to Saturday. We need to look at what happened to Christ's body in the Resurrection itself and the training and guidance needed to make it all happen.

Christ's Body

Christ's physical body was wrapped in a burial shroud and laid in a tomb. Some Christians today place misguided significance on this shroud, known as the "Shroud of Turin". It is important, but only in that it is a physical relic of what wrapped Jesus' physical body in death sleep.

The spirit, however, left the body. We remember Jesus' words: **"Father, into your hands I commend my spirit."** In this way, the spirit does not die. Not only does it not die, but it is given direction by Christ to go from the physical body and into the hands of God the Father.

The spirit then goes to be with God the Father. This must have been a relief for the spirit. An essence of pure light, massively bursting with truth, had been contained in a physical life body for 33 years. Imagine an elephant trying to sit in a mousehole, and you might begin to get an idea of what the spirit self of Christ had endured during His time on Earth.

While Jesus' spirit was on a journey and his lifeless, physical body was laid in the tomb, the Archangel Gabriel was stationed overhead. Although it is unclear if the Archangel Gabriel was there as a guard or as a watch–we do not know. He could have been there to protect the body against the forces of evil guided by Lucifer or Satan. Or he may have been waiting for his beloved master.

Satan and his accomplices are capable to steal or destroy the physical body even with guards present outside. Satan's powers are more than physical, he can change shape or manifest/unmanifest inside the tomb. Also, Satan is probably aware of Christ saying about 3rd day. So my personal opinion is that Archangel is present for protection.

There is evidence to suggest that Satan sided with the temple authorities to put Christ on the cross. Satan supported Christ's crucifixion. Satan is around and there is a possibility that he might steal the body if not protected. So it makes sense for God to appoint a guard in Archangel Gabriel over the tomb.

This would suggest that the Archangel Gabriel was actually standing guard instead of watching. If other heavenly beings are coming and going and are not subject to the awe and wonder of Christ's resurrection, then surely the Archangel Gabriel's purpose was more along the lines of a guard against the potential evil forces at work in opposition to God's will.

On Easter Saturday, the spirit returned to the tomb after spending time with God the Father. The spirit was not yet in the physical body, though it was present in the physical world and in the physical tomb.

Usually, the Seraphim beings transport the Soul to Heavenly worlds for the next phase of the journey. However, this was not the case with Christ; the heavenly beings came to the tomb to help if Christ needed it.

The Creator of the Universe is laid to rest, and it is the responsibility of the creatures of this world to care for their beloved creator. What an incredible and humble act God takes in this moment to trust creation to care for the Creator. Only through this time is resurrection possible.

Remembering Lazarus' Resurrection

This is not the first resurrection that happens. In John 11, we read of the death of Lazarus. His sisters, Mary and Martha, are distraught, and when Jesus comes back to town to visit his friends, they are upset with him for letting their brother die. Jesus is saddened by Lazarus' death, and we read the shortest sentence in Scripture: Jesus wept. (John 11:35)

Why would this make Jesus sad? He surely would have known the greater realities beyond the physical life world. It must be He loved Lazarus and did not want his to experience death without first knowing the possibilities of the true, spiritual Heaven that Christ reveals.

In this instance, it is revealed to us that Jesus did have the knowledge, insight, and command over the elements of the Universe that were of his own making. Remember, just because we refer to Jesus as "God the Son" does not mean He is not also God the Creator.

In Lazarus, we see the blueprint for Jesus' future resurrection that He carries out with His own body. Notice that Christ does not come to raise Lazarus on the first or second day after his death. It is, simply put, not possible when taking into account the process that we have outlined in the previous pages. The soul and spirit selves could not possibly be resurrected before the third day.

> In John 11:5-6, we read: "Accordingly, though Jesus loved Martha and her sister and Lazarus, after having heard that Lazarus was ill, he stayed two days longer in the place where he was." (NRSV)

Why else would Jesus have waited? It is clear it is not for want of love or compassion for Martha, Mary, or Lazarus. No! It is His understanding that for a resurrection to be possible, He must wait until at least the third day. In fact, Jesus waits until the fourth day before resurrecting Lazarus. "When Jesus arrived, he found that Lazarus had already been in the tomb for four days." (John 11:17)

There is some speculation as to why Jesus waited four days instead of three when it came to Lazarus. Some say that because this was Jesus' first resurrection, it took Him longer to perform that miracle. I do not think that is the case.

Although no one can be certain, the prevailing theory is that Lazarus, as a person accustomed to the physical body form, probably needed additional time for his soul and spirit life-forms to grasp what journey lay ahead of them. They were not pure light, and Lazarus could not have known beforehand what was in store for him. The extra day Jesus allowed for Lazarus was probably to account for the fact that it would take more time for his body to make the journey than Jesus' body would later take.

Christ's Soul Body Form

When it came to Christ's own resurrection, we must recall that Jesus chose to reside in a soul form body as it was more suitable for His mission. We cannot know for certain why He did this, but there are a few indicators that can help us in determining why this was the most appropriate course of action for Christ to take.

Upon returning to this physical, earthly world, Christ appears to nearly 1,000 people at various locations. This all happened in 40 short days, and we have to remember that Jesus would have been traveling on foot if He were required to be in His physical body. It just doesn't seem possible for Christ to have appeared to that many people in such a short time without the use of the soul bodily form and the advantages it has in being able to transcend the physical plane and transport the body to where it desires to be.

We know, however, through the story of Doubting Thomas, that there is enough of a body to actually be perceived in this world, which means that the form could not have been spiritual, as that form would be 100% light. Thomas is the one who asks to put his fingers in the holes of Jesus' hands where the nails went inserted. When Jesus returns, (by appearing in the middle of a room with a locked door nonetheless) He offers for Thomas to touch His body and feel the holes in His sides from where the spears went through. (John 20:24-29)

In such a brief example, we get a clear picture of the fact that Jesus did indeed have a soul-body after the Resurrection. He appears in the room because He can go through locked doors or walls by changing His frequency to be able to transcend the physical plane. He was then able to lower His frequency to be perceived by those who were in the locked room and could even allow them to touch the body if they chose.

The Process

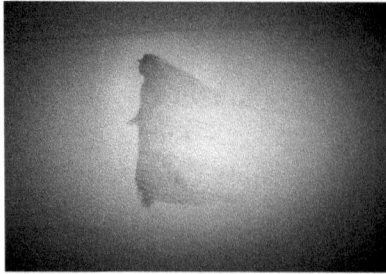

When a person dies in a 'normal' way, their soul is taken to the lower Heavenly worlds (also called Morontial worlds). In Jesus' case, this was not the case, a team of divine beings from Morontia worlds assembled under the direction of the Angel of Resurrection.

The Angel of Resurrection is Michael who was present along with a few other Morontia beings. The Angel of Resurrection is 100% light because he is a spiritual being. Remember, spirit life-forms can still be perceived and interact with heavenly worlds or physical realms, so the Angel of Resurrection is able to move and work across all realms through careful control of vibrations and frequencies.

In the case of Jesus, some beings from Heavenly (or Morontial) worlds came with midwayers to do what had already been decided. Midwayers are the closest persons to the third level of vibrations and include Archangels. These angels are present to assist if Christ needed it.

However, all indications are that Christ's Spirit was totally responsible to convert the physical body to light. This was the first step, and it was necessary because the spiritual self was the foundation for Christ's next step in His time on Earth. Previously, His physical body was the most necessary form, but for the time after the Resurrection, there was a different purpose to be fulfilled.

The transformation of the physical body to light became a sort of skeleton for the soul-body form. The soul body provided a shape for the total light physical body that contained the Spirit of Christ.

In essence, **Christ's body is a glorified form made up of both the lighted-physical-body encapsulated by the soul-body form.**

To be clear, although the Archangel of Resurrection offered training, the transitory experience of the Master as a personhood midway between the material and the spiritual was entirely through the power inherent in Christ. No being, Heavenly or otherwise, offered any sort of assistance. On his own, Jesus became a Soul-embodied being.

Jesus is unrecognizable by His closest followers after the Resurrection, so it has to be assumed that this soul-body did not appear to be physically similar to the body that Jesus had previously inhabited. A new body would account for the differences in ability and perception.

Once the body was ready, the physical linen wrappings were no longer needed. The linen clothes were neatly folded and kept at the head and feet of the tomb (John 20:7). Why is this detail shared? Why does it matter?

To be honest, I do not know if it has a huge significance. My estimation is that this is done on purpose to prove a point to humanity that there is an order and purpose to all things, even beyond death. Nothing is random. Just as hospital beds and clothes are folded by nurses and attendants, so, too, were these clothes folded by the midwayers who were present in the transformation of Christ. Their job was to help with the material things, and so they did just that.

The Training

Although Jesus the Christ is God the Eternal, there are still experiences that had been previously unknown to Him. Before coming to this earth, He did not know what it was like to experience life in human form. When He did come, He came as a baby, and like a baby, He learned to walk and talk. As Jesus grew up, He grew into his physical life body and became accustomed to it.

When Christ occupied a soul-body form, it was a completely new experience for Him. Unlike when He took the physical form of the baby, Jesus, He didn't have time to grow into this new body. Instead, He needed help, training, and guidance.

This is when the Archangel of Resurrection was particularly responsible in helping Christ to navigate this new body form. As the Chief of the Heavenly Morontial World, the Archangel of Resurrection was training Christ on how to use the body that was new to Him. Jesus needed instruction and training on how to control His vibrations.

In lowering the vibrations, the form would become visible to the human eye. When the vibrations increased, the form would no longer be sensed by human perspectives. The higher vibrational form was especially helpful when moving through walls or locked doors, as we saw when Jesus appeared to Thomas the Doubter.

While this would have been known for Jesus, it would still have required training and practice to perfect the abilities of this new body. The Archangel of Resurrection would have been the best teacher. All higher-level beings do these kinds of transformations when they come into contact with the physical human world. When you see the Archangel Gabriel appear in Scripture, it is because he has undergone this kind of change.

The training period continued through the whole day of Saturday and into Sunday morning.

When the women came to the tomb, although there are varying accounts, we do see them coming into contact with beings of light. In Mark's gospel and John's, we see an encounter with **"men in dazzling white."** These were beings of the Heavenly (or Morontial) world that were finishing up Jesus' training.

The idea these beings were perceived as men in dazzling white is because that is exactly how a human eye would perceive a Heavenly (or Morontial) being in training. Jesus is talking with these beings, and as Mary and the other women approach the tomb, they see the dazzling white men. They are not fully light, otherwise, they wouldn't be able to be seen by Mary. They are not fully physical, either, because then they would have appeared as physical humans and would not have been seen as 'dazzling'. It follows, then, that these beings were soul-embodied forms that were teaching Christ how to use the new body-form.

In the vast court of the resurrection halls of the first-heavenly world (or Morontial world), there may now be observed a magnificent, structure known as the "Christ Memorial", bearing the seal of the Archangel Gabriel, the chief executive for Christ. The Memorial was created shortly after Christ's departure from this world, and it bears this inscription: "In commemoration of the mortal transit of Jesus of Nazareth on Urantia."

Urantia, for those who may not understand, is another name for Earth. Universe knows Earth as Urantia as copyrighted in the universal records.

This is a memory that those beings do not want to miss. This transformation only happens once in the entirety of the Universe, and the beings who were present were quite blessed to be a part of it.

CONCLUSION

E aster symbolizes the Glorious Resurrection of Jesus Christ from death. This is the most important event in the history of Earth and is rightly celebrated around the world.

I sincerely hope this book has answered some of the questions surrounding Jesus' death and resurrection, including how and why the Resurrection took three days, what happened on Earth and in the Heavenly Realms while Jesus' body was in the tomb, and why Jesus chose to return as a soul life-form for the 40 days between resurrection and ascension.

At its core, Easter Saturday is when all of the work is done that we have come to celebrate on Easter Sunday. **There is no Sunday without Saturday**. Yes, it is good to celebrate the Resurrection on Easter Sunday, but the process of the Resurrection took more than just that one morning. Knowing that now, we can spend extra time in the study of these monumental events and in celebrating with wonder the process of the Creator.

He is Risen. He is Risen Indeed.

Happy Easter!

THANK YOU

I want to thank you personally for reading this book.

I have poured my Heart and Soul into these pages. I hope you have gained some valuable insights from the information presented. Please consider leaving your valuable review. Your review and feedback are important to me. Thank you so much.

Scan to write a review:

Preview from Book Lucifer Rebellion. Christ vs Satan – Final Battle for Earth has Begun

Chapter x – Clarion Call from GOD to all the Angels in Heaven

"What takes place on Earth is very important to Heaven." - Trinity Royal

In the previous chapters, you've learned about the spiritual forces at play throughout history and in the world right now. Even though they are unknown to the vast majority of humanity, you have chosen to open your eyes and discover how they have been and are influencing you and everyone around you. As Morpheus would say, You have taken the red pill.

With the knowledge you now possess, it is time to move on to more advanced topics where you will gain significantly more depth of knowledge. While you've learned about the spiritual Matrix, and how Dark-aligned and Light-aligned entities influence Earth–whether by enslaving humans or liberating them, encouraging selfishness rather than altruism, and so on, now you'll see specific instances of these activities–and the rationales behind specific plans launched by both sides in the war– especially centering around Jesus Christ and His teachings.

Why God Needs Your Help

We have seen in the previous chapters that the War came to be centered on planet Earth. Earth is the epicenter of the battle between Dark and Light. What happens here affects the rest of the Universe.

Due to this, the human race has become God's prized possession, and our planet Earth– also called Urantia in higher realms of consciousness–is the site of many of God's most important plans and a storehouse of His most valuable resources. For the purposes of this book, we don't need to go too far into the details of the Universal Father's creative activity, or every one of His agents. Here, we will simply go over the broadest, most basic points of Earth's history you need to know to get a grasp of what you need to do to help the forces of Light.

God's own son "the Son of God" is Christ, who is also the creator of the Universe. Millions of years ago, Christ manipulated many nebulae to form stars, and thus our galaxy, and around one of these stars at the edge of one of these galaxies is the Milky Way. Each galaxy consists of numerous solar systems and planets.

When our Creator created this planet, He noted that there was something special about this little blue orb, it became known as the "seed" planet. The seed planets are considered special as new souls are developed on these kinds of planets. The seed planets are the training ground for young Souls on an evolutionary path. There are very few in number in this part of our galaxy. Christ with the help of Trinity consciousness (God the Universal Father, Eternal, Son, and Infinite Spirit) created the Human species. So we are created in His "likeness" as the scriptures state, making the residents of our planet particularly important for the plans of both God and Satan.

Human beings evolved empathy, compassion, altruism, and especially religious feelings much earlier in our development than was the case for sentient beings in other worlds. As a result, the spiritual energies produced by the development of human souls, whether ascending towards higher consciousness realms as the Light desires or chained down to this lower dimensional consciousness as the Dark desires, far outweigh those produced by even heavenly beings in the universe. Since the war has been at a stalemate in the rest of the Universe for a very long time, with neither Lucifer's forces nor the Light has been able to dislodge the other, Earth has taken center stage as the decisive point. Darkness, unfortunately, has managed to make significant in-roads on our planet and has advanced its plans very far. On the other hand, the Universal Father has plans of his own involving His most powerful agent here: Jesus Christ, whom we shall learn more about in future chapters. This should suffice as an overview of the Universal Father treasures humanity in particular so much.

Effects of the Rebellion

Now, due to Lucifer's rebellion, discussed in previous chapters, God has had a very difficult time reaching out to humanity, protecting and guiding us, despite how highly He valued us. The path for growth toward the Light was growing harder and harder for us, with many obstacles placed in our way. Here are some of the ways Darkness has interfered with us:

- No real religious teachings. There have been many great religions started by enlightened prophets which have been stamped out by the Dark. Humanity has been made to forget these religions and their teachings to delay the growth of many strong souls and prevent knowledge about the great spiritual conflict from spreading widely.

- Manipulation of teachings. Cunning agents of Darkness have manipulated some teachings of religions throughout history–and in the present day–to sow confusion and make it even harder for seekers to attain genuine knowledge of Heaven and higher spiritual realms.

- Over-emphasis on the process: Partially due to machinations from the Dark, but also due to honest mistakes which built up over time, much of humanity has become too focused on ritual–rather than finding their own individual "spark" of God within themselves.

Finally, whereas direct communication with God is possible on higher realms that are more vibrationally attuned to Paradise–the Veil or Matrix which envelopes Earth has cut us off from the Divine in some way. Only if we are very fortunate can some of us access higher realities, and often only in dreams; communion with the Universal Father Himself is very rare, with only the Bestowal of Christ giving us hope (described in the next chapter).

Even so, there are some agents of the Light who have come to Earth to assist us in reaching higher consciousness levels, even if they were not in direct contact with the Divine. Some gods in ancient polytheistic or henotheistic religions were heavenly messengers who came to help Humanity in the evolution process. Also religious figures like Lord Buddha or Lord Krishna, philosophers like Aristotle, Plato, Zeno of Elea, Confucius, and some modern-day personages like Martin Luther King. Some angels even gave inspiration to great inventors and teachers, like Jonas Salk–creator of the polio vaccine, Albert Einstein, and other Nobel Prize winners.

All these people were sent or influenced by the Light to guide mankind towards the climactic event which will occur soon, in the present time we are living in. The Dark has also influenced our world in many ways, both enslaving individual humans, trapping their souls, encouraging the evolution of dark cults, and, teaching other individuals selfish methods of increasing their power and influence. Some Dark agents manifested in this world directly, putting on human disguises, while others merely contacted ordinary people seeking power and subtly guided them into the shadows. Many Dark agents or servants settled as kings, queens, or great and bloody conquerors. Adolf Hitler and Ghenghis Khan are two such examples. Less famously, Dark agents generally tried-and are still trying-to infiltrate large, powerful, centralized governments to control information and how people lived, to ensure as few as possible could ascend. They also manipulate the genetic code of humanity, to cut out strands of DNA carrying Light codes-such as nobler, more altruistic temperaments, higher attunement to spiritual realities, a higher propensity to dream-and so on.

Despite both sides doing their best throughout hundreds of thousands of years, Light was never able to break Dark's grasp on the world, and Dark could never remove every trace of Light from Earth, even as its influence steadily grew. Thus, the war on Earth was grinding down into a stalemate as well; whatever advantages Dark had would take many, many centuries to come to fruition. Before that can happen, the forces of Light desire to strike a shattering blow against Satan/Lucifer. The fallen Morning Star, cunning as he is, anticipated that, and is attempting to gather his forces for his decisive annihilation of Light on Earth, which will allow him to capture the planet and turn all of the prodigious energy humans produce into his ends.

God's Counterattack

As the situation on Earth is rapidly heating up, the Universal Father focused more and more of His energies and attention on it. About 200,000 years ago, He made a clarion call to all of His angels to focus on humanity and do all they can to uplift the consciousness of this blue orb. God is no fool and made clear to His angelic forces that this would likely be the most difficult mission they had ever attempted ever in their entire existence. God also emphasized to them this struggle was worth it, for He realized how unique and powerful humanity is due to its peculiar evolutionary history, and thus He loves humanity and Earth more than any other place in the Universe. Much of God's focus is on humanity and earth at the present time. This is an absolute fact.

This clarion call rang out wide to all of Heavens and Paradise. The mission was simply to save Humans and Earth. A mission like this was never attempted in the history of creation.

Since this was unique, a vast number of angels had no idea what to expect and did not sign up for the mission. Given the incredible skills, the angels possessed, very many of them could not take it for fear of the unknown. Many were afraid of the struggle and Satan's forces in general and were also uncertain of the outcome. Most have already witnessed the devastation caused by Lucifer's rebellion in the Heavens. After all, such an endeavor had never been attempted before, and no histories existed in the great archives and annals of Heaven that could give any guidance on a war like this. The angels who raised these concerns did not have full faith in the Universal Father's victory, so they chose to sit out the battle and wait and see who would win. Others did not want to limit their consciousness by focusing on one planet in one system in one planet of the vast Universe.

In fairness to these seemingly cowardly angels, fighting Satan's forces on Earth is a truly monumental task. The Matrix surrounding Earth has several characteristics that make things harder for the Light than the Dark.

However, some angels did have faith in God and Christ and said "yes" to this divine mission. There were at least 144,000 of these according to the Holy Bible. These are the angles who have agreed to come into the Matrix and be part of the Matrix, mingle with evolving Human souls, and increase the vibrations of Human consciousness thereby helping God and the cause of light. These angels were known as descended angels. According to a divinely orchestrated plan, these brave angelic souls planted themselves at predetermined strategic points of Human evolution to become teachers, preachers, inventors, gurus, sadhus, scientists..etc. Basically to teach and help evolve Humanity.

> Then I looked, and behold, the Lamb was standing on Mount Zion, and with Him one hundred and forty-four thousand, having His name and the name of His Father written on their foreheads. – Revelations 14:1

However life is not all rosy for these brave angels; by being in the Matrix, all of them got caught up in the illusion of the Matrix, and most if not all forgot their divine origins and inter-mingled with humans over the period of 200,000 years. This has helped to manipulate the DNA of the Human species, thereby evolving the human species faster and closer to God. If Light wins, these brave angels will enjoy all the splendor and accolades they have earned.

The Matrix prevents spiritual beings from heavenly realms from passing into Earth. They are only allowed in if a resident of Earth, within the Matrix itself, specifically asks them to enter. This is called the doctrine of non-interference. Some beings can get around this, but it is extremely rare, and Dark forces like demons and shadow-whisperers more often do this. The great Bestowal of Christ was one exception to this rule in Light's favor. Another exception was the case of 'original seeders,' angels who visited humanity in distant past eons to place Light information in our genomes.

The effects of the Matrix on the development of the soul itself present another obstacle to the cause of Light due to loss of memory. Souls, ignorant as they are, cannot easily coordinate with each other, or angelic beings, and must rely on their internal abilities to evolve, which can be made easier if the bodies to which they are reincarnated possess useful strands of Light-aligned DNA. In this regard, humans possessing these types of DNA should mingle as much as possible with the rest of the human population to spread them far and wide and to future generations, but again, since accumulated knowledge is lost, this is harder to do. Souls must also learn their own lessons, rather than being taught, how to avoid the pitfalls of the Dark, transform Dark energies into Light ones, and enhance the collective consciousness of humanity.

Given all this, you can imagine why God is personally concerned with this war on a single small planet and refuses to give up on the human race. It is extremely important for Him and the Light to win this war, as so many of His strongest angels have already invested so much. In other words, not only are human souls at stake, but Paradise and other types of angels from higher heavenly realms also have vulnerable souls that might be at risk if they lose. Thus, God has a vested interest in you—yes, you! He wants your soul to grow, advance, and improve your spiritual life so you can help in the struggle. This will determine whether Light or Dark wins in the end.

I am certain you will love the rest of the book. Here is the link

PREVIEW FROM BOOK - SON OF MAN BECOMES SON OF GOD

"The reason the Son of God appeared was to destroy the Devil's work." -Ephesians 6:12

First Coming Mission - Fight the Devil

I t was one of the greatest battles in the history of humanity and the planet Earth itself. The fate of Earth, and many worlds beyond it, hinged upon its outcome. Yet it was not fought with swords and shields, nor bullets and tanks. One side did not even take up arms. It was not a physical struggle. And most of all, absolutely no one except its participants witnessed its progress and ultimate outcome, even though all of history would have been radically different if the other side had won.

It was rather a struggle purely on the moral plane—the temptation of Christ, where the forces of Darkness tried and failed to turn our Savior over to them and convince Him to reject the Universal Father. It is certainly good they failed or else we likely wouldn't be here—or we would perhaps be suffering fates worse than death! But how did this moral struggle play out? It is easy to visualize great battles with weapons and soldiers, but a purely spiritual conflict seems a great deal harder to wrap one's head around. This chapter will tell you everything you need to know about the temptation of Christ.

Testing is part of the process of the Spiritual Journey

Every human being, young and old, male or female, from any part of the world, has to deal with challenges in their life. We all also have to make choices and, in many cases, resist temptation. Sometimes we have to choose between an action pleasurable in the short-term and another more profitable in the long-term, or between actions that could hurt others but benefit us personally, or those which require sacrifice on our part but benefit society as a whole.

The most significant and best-remembered stories often involve choices like these, and these themes also show up in the great religions of the world, capturing universal truths as they do.

Testing is important for one's soul because it proves you have truly learned all you can on the lower levels, thus allowing you to move on to higher consciousness levels safely. Again, take the analogy of a high school or college course. You certainly wouldn't take the final exam on the very first day of class, but you wouldn't take it even in the first week or month either. Instead, you'd first take smaller quizzes, and then a midterm, only building up to the final exams gradually. The same applies to spiritual matters. First, your soul undergoes minor trials, with the hope that you will learn and grow from them. Finally, at the very end, you will have to endure a "Dark Night of the Soul", all by yourself, with no aid or assistance this time, in order to demonstrate you've truly internalized all the lessons of your previous struggles and can apply those lessons in a coherent and cumulative way. Christ's spiritual test on Hermon was the greatest of this kind imaginable. Instead of just struggling with internal vices like most humans do in their soul journeys, He faced down the leaders of darkness themselves, drawing upon the lessons He had gained from childhood and young manhood—the love of His parents and friends, His struggles with smaller physical inconveniences like stomach ailments or falling down, and so on—and proved he could utilize all those lessons in an arena where God was on the sidelines

All in all, this was Christ's personal test to prove Him to be a worthy Creator Son and ruler over the entire universe. This sort of thing is analogous to the smaller tests all human beings go through, both in mundane terms and higher spiritual ones. When you're in school, you're expected to pass your math, history, and other courses with tests and exams, which you have to take all by yourself with no external aid. Someone helping you during the test itself, or you looking at someone else's answers, would be cheating! The same applies to a spiritual journey. When you want to demonstrate the advancement of your intellectual and moral abilities, you have to do so entirely on your own, without any direct aid from God or higher spiritual entities, to prove that you are the one who has advanced and that you, on your own, are capable of advanced spiritual work, rather than needing to rely on others all the time. Only then will you be permitted to grow to higher planes of c onsciousness.

Soul progression happens only with testing

Just as students go from one class to the other through passing examinations, life will always bring tests to us when it is time for us to move forward. Tests are not something that our fleshly nature wants, there is always a conflict between our body and the structures that God had prepared for our progressions and achievements in life. It is another way of building and strengthening us from within. The universe is always in a conspiracy for our growth.

Passing spiritual tests with little or no support

There are times when loyalty to God will be driven out from within us. Even for Jesus Christ, there needed to be pressure upon the flesh to drive out the possibilities of the Spirit. It might not be suitable to go through trials and difficulties in life, but it is a sure way to help us realize the possibilities that are secretly embedded in us. The same applied to Christ, though it was much more significant for Him than it would be for an ordinary person taking the SATs or something, of course.

For Christ's test on Mount Hermon, at the moment of Satan's temptation, the Universal Father temporarily left Him, as did all the guardian angels who were protecting Him previously. In that sense, Christ was totally alone, as one might have to take the SATs alone. However, Christ was not left entirely powerless. His spirit had certain kinds of astral and etheric protection in place that the guardian angels had left behind so that the forces of Darkness could not use any unfair methods to simply mind-control Him or bend Him to their will. But aside from that, He had nothing except His own wisdom and knowledge of God to refute the lies of the darkness.

Evolved beings usually have suffered more

Some people love to put it as suffering while others love to put it as challenges; whichever way you put it, they are like the grease that makes our movement easy from one stage of purpose fulfillment to the other. This is proof that the wisdom of God is foolishness to man, we don't want to suffer, and we don't like having challenges. We are not happy when we are being tried, we respond by crying, and some of us even tend to blame God for our ordeals. Leaving God to seek help from other means is the worst-case scenario. Challenges are promotions in disguise; only those who have been through one can understand. Even nature explains to us how important it is to suffer before we eventually begin to bear fruits. It has been proven by many lives also that the deeper the suffering is, the greater the glory to come. This is why we must not compare ourselves with anyone irrespective of how close we are to them.

A superhero journey

Can you imagine any real superhero who did not go through their Dark Night of the Soul? I do not think there is any.

What qualifies a superhero? When you hear the word superhero, you might look at some who have all the material, but superheroes are those who have been tested and proven. A superhero is known for how many inner battles he has conquered and how he has been able to find strength from within to stand for the truth even if there are a lot of pressures around. Superheros are known for their maturity, resilience, strength, and many other virtues that have been gained during tests. Everyone goes through dark nights, but how we deal with them or our actions makes our character and hence shapes our destiny.

Universe Trial

Christ closed Himself off spiritually to all other distractions, but for only communion with The Father. He went through five weeks of intense training. This was His "Dark Night of the Soul". What exactly the training entails in this five weeks is not generally public knowledge at this time and is beyond the scope of discussion for this short book.

After five weeks of this training, despite the hunger His human body endured, Jesus was more assured and self-confident than ever before. He knew He had gained as much wisdom and understanding as it was possible to acquire on the mortal plane of this universe, and was certain he had triumphed over the most basic material levels of this particular personality manifestation in this specific region of space-time.

In the sixth week of the journey, the very last, Jesus knew it was time for his greatest trial. This event in the universal records came to be known as the "Universe Trail". This was the very reason He has chosen to come to this planet.

At the end of his self-imposed exile, he opened Himself spiritually to worldly distractions. The leaders of the Darkness, Satan, and his allies descended physically to Mount Hermon and could be seen with the naked eye by Jesus. They also sent many of their demonic servants physically to attack and harass Him.

Satan and his allies were able to manifest and un-manifest their body in physical form, meaning they had a body form and the knowledge to use this body form. However, Jesus' body form is limited to physical form and does not have the ability to manifest and un-manifest at will in the physical realm. This is important to know because Dark forces had greater power to affect material beings. However, they were not able to cause harm to Jesus, as he is protected and also has the 'awareness' and abilities to protect himself.

After the demons could not even come close to breaking Christ physically or mentally, Satan tried to subvert Christ spiritually, through the temptations described in the Bible.

The Tests

Indeed, the temptation itself recapitulated the slow increase of difficulty one might experience in the aforementioned examples, but this time pertaining to levels of spirit and mind in addition to the complexity of the subject matter. It is not an accident that Satan posed precisely three questions to Christ. These questions were designed to test the multiple components of the soul, starting with the lowest human ego first, and then going from that to the higher self. The devil knew what he wanted to achieve, but had to be cunning because that is his nature. The test he put Christ through was to prove that no man was above mistakes and that Jesus Christ was also subject to the flesh.

Satan is aware of Christ's divine status. However, Satan thinks that Christ does not know Himself. So he prefixed the questions with "If you are the Son of God" for the first two questions. Also, Satan thought that the person on the mountain does not know him, so in the last question when Christ answered by calling Satan by name, Satan's cover is blown off.

Test-1: Testing physical body weakness, immediate human gratification with physical food.

> And the tempter came and said to him, "If you are the Son of God, command these stones to become loaves of bread." – Mathew 4:3

Tempting Christ with bread—was purely physical, and measured His resistance to immediate gratification. This is the lowest, most animalistic part of the human psyche.

After all, even the most basic animals incapable of any sort of higher thought, like slugs or sessile creatures like coral, still need food in the form of nutrition. This was accordingly the easiest test to pass for any enlightened creature, since control over one's bodily functions and urges is one of the first things required to pass from infancy to childhood to adulthood, and thus one of the first marks of true sapience. Jesus was too savvy for this ploy.

> He replied, "It is written: 'Man shall not live on bread alone, but on every word that comes from the mouth of God.'" – Mathew 4:4

Test-2: Testing of divine nature - If he jumped from a cliff, will angels catch him?

> "If you are the Son of God, throw yourself down, for it is written, "'He will command his angels concerning you,' and "'On their hands they will bear you up, lest you strike your foot against a stone.'" - Mathew 4:6

The test is challenging Christ to attempt suicide so that angels would assumedly rescue Him, reflecting a high level of human consciousness: our ability to trust in God. Lower animals do not truly understand the existence of higher spiritual realities, though they do have a vague awareness of them (see, for instance, how dogs often seem sensitive to ghosts and demons). Only rational creatures, most notable humans on Earth, are capable of consciously acknowledging God's existence and carrying out His will. In Christ's case, His divine nature would have also reflected His knowledge of divine commands, so this was a test for that supernaturally high level of Christ's spirit, which most human beings in ordinary life lack. The fact that Christ did not feel the need to jump from the top of the temple proved He had total trust and faith in God, and thus proved He was entirely aware of His true nature, His mission, and the ultimate good that would come of God's plans.

Jesus maintained his integrity and responded by quoting scripture, saying, "It is said, Thou shalt not tempt the Lord thy God.'" - Matthew 4:7

Test-3: Testing of Human Ego, Power - Satan offers Christ to become the prince of the planet if he bows

Satan has the power to manifest and unmanifest at will. Satan led Jesus to the highest point in the land, Mount Hermon, and with his supernatural powers, showed Him in a single instant every kingdom on Earth that existed at the moment and would exist in the future.

Satan told Jesus, "I will give you all their authority and splendor; it has been given to me, and I can give it to anyone I want to. If you worship me, it will be all yours."

The test involved a higher level of human consciousness as well: Our desire for power, influence, and fame, which is an outgrowth of our nature as social creatures, or our human ego. The natural man is prone to pride and creates in all of us a desire for recognition, power, and riches. Not only do these seem to provide easy solutions to life's many problems, but they also seem to fill our need to feel important and loved. Individuals, families, and nations have gone to the ends of the earth and their beliefs to earn more money and gain more glory. The test for power comes to every man in life. It does not matter who that man is; as long as one is human, there will always be a need to acquire or fight for power. Power is in different phases and various parts of life. There is the power to rule; there is power brought about by monetary possessions, there is power brought about by intellectualism, and all forms of power are worth fighting for. Power makes everyone around us see us as important, and after acquiring everything we need, the quest for power is a natural feeling that comes to us; the ability to make sure that we do not become too obsessive about it is what we all need as humans. It is a natural thing to desire power, but time and conditions are what help us to decipher whether it is right for us or not.

The very lowest creatures do not possess egos because they have no social relations at all. Slugs live more and less by themselves, except for mating, and they do not form parental bonds, they just leave their eggs where they lay them. Coral and other sessile creatures can't move or experience things at all, so naturally, they do not possess anything even close to an ego. Animals that live in herds and flocks, where they have to help each other survive, are more complex and thus have primitive egos, but the ego is most thoroughly developed in humankind, where we must always navigate the complexities of human society: worrying about how various groups perceive us, our material standing in relation to those groups, what courtesy requires towards all of them, and so on. Because of these social relations, we are always thinking about fame and power, and that is the biggest challenge for our ego; we must learn to subsume such 'egoistic' desire to our faith in God.

Christ succeeded perfectly in this. Becoming prince of Earth, as Satan offered, would be nearly irresistible to the social ego on its own, but Christ knew better and promptly refused Satan's offer with His apt and witty response

> "Away from me, Satan! For it is written: 'Worship the Lord your God, and serve him only.' – Mathew 4:10

The Aftermath of Satan's Tests

Some of us might wonder why Satan stopped after just three questions. He is certainly a persistent and devious Lord of Darkness, after all. Would he really have given up so easily? And were there really only three temptations that could have possibly worked against Christ?

Perhaps Christ put a stop to all of Satan's schemes (at that moment) with His answer to the third question. Christ ended the whole conversation with "Away from me, Satan!" implying that Christ recognized Satan and commanded authoritatively. This must have been a shock to Satan as he did not expect it."

If the only thing Christ said was 'no' that probably would have encouraged Satan to keep going, dragging out the test longer than it needed to be. But with an authoritative statement of God's ultimate lordship, Christ proved there was nothing those two could possibly say to convince Him. That would have been enough to get Satan to shut up and realize that the Dark had thoroughly lost that battle.

Now, the Bible does not record what Satan said in response to that. Luke only states that the devil "left him until an opportune time" (NIV Luke 4:13). Perhaps Satan simply fled, struck speechless and in utter fear by the glory of the Lord. However, it is more likely that Satan left Christ with an "open invitation," given that he was said to have been waiting for an opportune time in the future. In other words, Satan might have said something like, "We will always be ready for you if you choose to join us in the future." Even if he failed at the moment, Satan probably hoped that the subversion would succeed at a later date, if he managed to sow doubt into Christ's heart. That obviously did not happen, and again, this is complete speculation due to the dangers of research into Dark plans and motives. There may well be many other possibilities, but these hypotheses are intended simply to expand the reader's horizons and make him or her think, not proclaim unshakeable religious tr uth.

Overall, this was a massive blow to Darkness' plans and a strong repudiation of the dark manifesto. Without Christ on their side, Satan and his dark minions no longer had any hope of drawing Earth into their orbit entirely unopposed, though they would of course continue to subvert it over the millennia. However, with Christ spreading His moral teachings far and wide, their attempts would be greatly stymied. By the same token, Christ's loyalty to God disproved many elements of Satan's manifesto, such as his claims that the Universal Father was not fit to rule, that the residents of the universe should not follow Him and should instead focus on service to self rather than others—though of course under Satan's dominion anyways. By rejecting Satan's temptations without any help or external influences, Jesus proved that the path of righteousness, narrow though it may be, could still triumph and, thus, that Satan's promises of freedom and 'self-determination' from God's rule were empty and false.

Return from the Wilderness

And as we have seen, Christ rejected every one of the temptations the evil forces threw at Him. Thanks to that, when the evil ones were finally forced to flee at the end of the sixth week, the entire universe recognized that Christ and only Christ were worthy to lead it.

Satan's great, sneaky plan had failed utterly, and he had to retreat from Earth in rage and shame. He certainly did not give up: Luke notes he left Jesus "until an opportune time," and indeed we know now that he is still carrying out spiritual warfare and all sorts of sly machinations to undermine Christ and the Father's will, and to also lead humanity into darkness, to this very day. Nevertheless, in that particular moment in time over two thousand years ago, Satan found he had nothing more in his bag of tricks that could possibly separate Christ and the Father, thus allowing the forces of Light to enjoy a well-earned victory. Indeed, even though he had been starving for forty days, Christ returned from Mount Hermon rejuvenated and even more powerful than before; Luke describes Him returning to Galilee "in the power of the Spirit," where the entire region started talking about Him and praising His wisdom and power (NIV, Luke 4:14 – 30).

By staying loyal to the will of His Father, Christ showed that it was possible for individuals of goodwill to stand up for what is right and spurn the false and selfish promises Dark tricksters offer. He proved He was capable of administering the universe justly and kindly, without concern for His own self-interest, and thus protecting all of its residents from Lucifer/Satan's rebellion—and any future rebellions that may occur.

Basking in the glow of victory, Christ went down from Mount Hermon. He met the boy who helped Jesus prior to his journey up the mountain. He told him only one important sentence:

> "The period of rest is over, I must return to my Father's business!"

The boy understood that Christ's mission now took Him far beyond what a normal human being could endure.

Jesus Himself had definitely changed: In addition to His newfound confidence, He was much quieter, almost silent when He was not preaching because the duties as a protector of the entire universe weighed so heavily on Him. He began the next phase of the Father's plan for the salvation of Earth—and by extension all of the Universe.

The testing marked the end of His purely human career and the beginning of the more divine phase of His Bestowal.

Son of Man becomes Son of GOD

When Christ went up the mountain:

- He was a Son of Man when he walked up the mountain with all limitations and fragileness of human

- He was confused and not sure what God wanted of Him

- He was in deep introspection

- He did not know how and when to start his public mission

- He was introverted and not able to share His Father, the divine with-in message, and good news with others

- He had a lot of questions about his divine nature and the purpose of his bestowal

- He knew He had to face the dark lord head-on that ravaged His creation. He was fragile and unsure of how things would unfold

When Christ came down the mountain:

- He is completely sure of Himself and of what God wanted from Him

- He is no longer in deep introspection

- He knew that it is time for Him to start his mission in the public

- He got all answers to all his questions about his divine nature and the purpose of his bestowal

- He came back fully confident, basking in the glory of God and with great power and authority over the entire planet and the entire universe

- He is now ready to share His Father, the divine with-in message, and good news to all who have ears to hear

- He successfully defeated the dark Lord and displaced the dark planetary prince.

I am certain you will love the rest of the book. Here is the link:

SON OF MAN becomes SON OF GOD

TRINITY ROYAL

Scan Me

Welcome to Heaven. Your Graduation from Kindergarten Earth to Heaven

"I go and prepare a place for you, I will come back and take you to be with me that you also may be where I am." - John 14:3

Ever wonder **if Heaven is real**? What **proof** do we have?

How does one **go to Heaven**? What are the **minimum requirements for Heaven**?

Why <u>**Life of Earth is your Kindergarten school**</u>?

Trinity explores the following:

- Isn't Heaven **just a mind concept**? *What is the proof of its existence? Why do I even bother about Heaven? What is in it for me?*

- What are the **minimum requirements to go to Heaven or the ticket booth to Heaven**?

- *Why is life on Earth your* **kindergarten school**?

- Are there **different levels to heaven? If so, how many? What are they?** Does the **time and space continuum exist in Heaven?** *If so how different is it compared to Earth's time and space?*

Your Life in Heaven. Family, Marriage, Sex, Work

"No eye has seen, no ear has heard, and no mind has imagined what God has prepared for those who love him." – 1 Corinthians 2:9

Ever wonder what your **life in Heaven will look like after your mortal death**?

Is there **Marriage** in Heaven? Do you have a **Family in Heaven**?

Do you have your **Parents or kids or your siblings** in Heaven?

Do you have **Sexual intercourse** in Heaven?

And what do you do all day? Is there a **daily Job**? Oh. And will you meet your **deceased family members**, friends, and relatives?

These are questions that curious minds like me ask. You will find **authoritative un-speculated** answers here.

SOS - Save yOur Soul

"For what shall it profit a man, if he shall gain the whole world, and lose his own soul?" - Mark 8:36

Ever Wonder **What Happens After You Die**? Is it the end?

What did **Christ** Say about death and life after mortal death?

Is there a way to Save yOur Soul? If so How?

What exactly is **Soul** and **Spirit**, is it just a new age concept? What did Christ Say?

Trinity considered to be one of the bridges between Heaven and Earth, shares general Angelic knowledge. This book explores:

What are the unseen parts of us that make us who we are? What is left behind after Mortal death and what happens to these **unseen parts of us**?

What exactly is **Soul** and **Spirit**, is it just a new age concept? What did Christ Say? Is there a way to Save yOur Soul? If so How? Does Heaven actually exist? Can a ticket to Heaven be guaranteed?

Lucifer Rebellion. Christ vs. Satan – Final Battle for Earth Has Begun

Multiple Award-winning Book

"extraordinary book" "Definitely a five-star read" - [International Review of Books]

Ever wonder **why there is a War between GOD and the Devil?** Ever wonder how the **War in Heaven started or what the Lucifer Rebellion is**?

Ever wonder why War in heaven came to Earth or why darkness still exists on Earth? And why did God send Christ to Earth?

This book explores:

- How and Why did the **war in Heaven start**? How did the War in Heaven come to Earth?
- Why did **God send Christ** to planet Earth? Was it to save Humanity and the Universe?
- What exactly happened during **Christ's First Coming** event? What is expected during the Second Coming event?

Trinity takes us on a **journey beyond time and space** to find the answers to these questions that every believer should know.

Lucifer Rebellion. Christ vs Satan – The Second Coming of Christ

Scan Me

Ever wonder **why there is a War between GOD and Devil?**

Ever wonder how the **War in Heaven started or what Lucifer Rebellion is?** **and why War in Heaven came to Earth** and why darkness still exists on Earth?

This book explores:

- How and Why did the **war in Heaven start**?

- How did the War in Heaven come to Earth?

- Why did **God send Christ** to planet Earth? Was it to save Humanity and the Universe?

- What are the effects of War on Earth and in Heaven?

- What exactly happened during **Christ's First Coming** event?

- What is expected during the Second Coming event?

I invite you to join me on a journey beyond space and time when the Lucifer Rebellion started and the reasons for Christ's First and Second Coming events.

Christ & Demons - Unseen Realms of Darkness

"The reason the Son of God appeared was to destroy the Devil's work." -Ephesians 6:12

Is there an **UNSEEN world of Darkness** hidden in front of our eyes?

Ever wonder why **Evil** exists on Earth? Ever wonder how **Satan got to planet Earth a**nd what exactly is the Dark Empire Agenda?

Ever wonder why Christ chose planet Earth for His great Bestowal?

What is the **agenda of Darkness**? Why do God and Christ let dark forces flourish on Earth? Does God have a plan? What is it?

What are the differences between **Demons, Evil Spirits, and Ghosts**? How does **Selling one's Soul to the devil** happen?

Son of Man becomes Son of God. One Event that Changed the History of the World

<u>Award-Winning Book</u>

"*an opportunity for the reader to embark on a journey with Him, feel what He feels*"

"*A fascinating description and story of how Christ emerged, changed and developed into the highest of holiest beings, second only to God.*"

"*An exceptional and well-written novel without the preaching and pointless prose and verbiage of others of this type*"

There is **ONE event** that is the true turning point in the history of Earth. This is not the Birth or Baptism of Jesus, but it is the **fight with the Devil**

Ever wonder what would have happened to Earth if Christ failed against Satan? This was a real possibility, although it is considered blasphemous to talk about it.

From Suffering to Healing

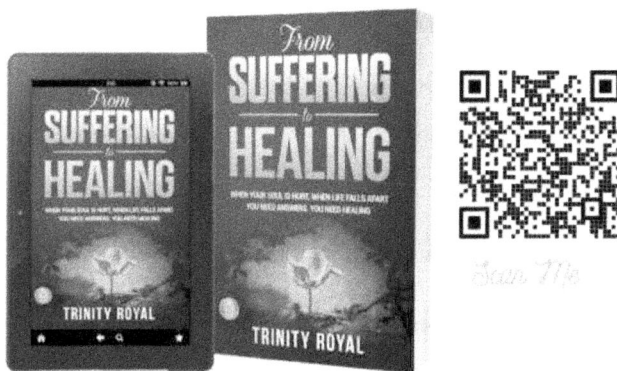

"I highly recommend this for anyone *who has ever suffered in their lives*, and, in all honesty, who hasn't?"

Why do **bad things happen to good people**?

Why does your **Life journey lead you to suffer?**

The Answer is to Heal You.

Your suffering is the epitome of a **blessing in disguise.** Wrapped in darkness and suffering, it removes the ground from beneath your feet and leaves you fearful, fragile, and devoid of meaning in life.

Most beings that we adore or worship have gone through dark times in their life. This includes Christ, Buddha, Gandhi, Nelson Mandela, Oprah, Abraham Lincoln, etc. This process is necessary as it redefines a person, re-makes one character, and chips away the darkness to bring out the luster of your **Real Self.** This is your **METAMORPHOSIS.**

Dark Night of the Soul

Award-Winning Book

Our wounds are often the openings into the best and the most beautiful parts of us." -David Richo

Ever wonder **why suffering happens for no known reason...**

Ever wonder **why your Soul is longing...**

Have you ever felt like you have a **splinter in your mind, that does not let you off the hook..**

If so, **you are chosen for a purpose. There is GOD's hand working in your life.**

While there are many reasons people suffer (most are self-made or bad decisions or external in nature); the type of Suffering referred to as the "Dark Night of the Soul" has a clear and definite purpose. **The purpose is your Soul's growth.**

Your Answers and Healing await. Click on Buy Now.

Free books to our readers

War in Heaven came to Earth. Satan Rebellion:

https://dl.bookfunnel.com/ea12ys3dmk

Your Life in Heaven:

https://dl.bookfunnel.com/vg451qpuzs

GLOSSARY

Glossary

Apostle: One sent by Christ to spread His work and word in this world.

Archangel: In angelic hierarchy, an archangel is a heavenly being of the highest rank.

Canonical Gospels: The gospels that we see included in the canon of the Bible (Matthew, Mark, Luke, and John). These gospels are what early church fathers agreed upon as being accurate and true to the faith. There are other, noncanonical gospels (Thomas, Mary, etc.) that are not included in our research here.

Disciple: A follower of Jesus Christ, usually a reference to the 12 original disciples.

Morontia: Also known as the "soul life-form", the morontia is the form between the physical body we occupy now and the final form of a spirit body. It has higher vibration frequencies than a physical body but lower frequencies than a spiritual body.

Morontial Plane: The plane of existence for soul life-forms. It is a step closer to the center of Heaven than this physical realm.

Paradise Isle: Where God resides and is 100% light.

Salvington: The headquarters of the Universe.

Sanhedrin: High council of Jewish priests at the time of Jesus' death, including the high priest, Caiaphas.

Seraphim: An angelic being that is very high in the hierarchy of ordered angels. It is winged, and in the course of resurrection, is tasked with caring for the body in transition.

Urantia: Other name for Earth used in the universe.

References

References

English Standard Version Bible. (2001). ESV Online.

Did Jesus really resurrect? (2021, April 2). Urantia Foundation.

New Revised Standard Version. (2019). Oremus.org. https://bible.oremus.org/

Christ vs Satan – Final Battle for Earth has Begun - https://books2read.com/b/TheRealMatrix

Image References

https://pixabay.com/photos/resurrection-of-jesus-christ-painting-4627099/. (n.d.)

.https://pixabay.com/photos/statues-pierre-update-tomb-jesus-5027619/. (n.d.).

About Author

Trinity is a multi-award-winning author and a spiritual warrior. While life might not always work out according to plan, Trinity was able to take valuable lessons from each new experience. Trinity grew and developed and now shares a passion for enlightening others on spiritual knowledge in the hopes of closing the gap between Heaven and Earth. Trinity's writings reflect the depths of a passion and desire to connect with everyone seeking spiritual growth and education.

You can learn more at www.RocketshipPath2God.com or @ https://www.facebook.com/TrinityRoyalBooks

www.ingramcontent.com/pod-product-compliance
Lightning Source LLC
LaVergne TN
LVHW020055090426
835513LV00029B/1804